THE GREATER MEKONG SUBREGION ECONOMIC COOPERATION PROGRAM STRATEGIC FRAMEWORK 2030

SEPTEMBER 2021

© 2021 Asian Development Bank
6 ADB Avenue, Mandaluyong City, 1550 Metro Manila, Philippines
Tel +63 2 8632 4444; Fax +63 2 8636 2444
www.adb.org

Some rights reserved. Published in 2021.

ISBN 978-92-9262-689-1 (print), 978-92-9262-690-7 (electronic), 978-92-9262-691-4 (ebook)
Publication Stock No. TCS210042
DOI: http://dx.doi.org/10.22617/TCS210042

The views expressed in this publication are those of the authors and do not necessarily reflect the views and policies of the Asian Development Bank (ADB) or its Board of Governors or the governments they represent.

ADB does not guarantee the accuracy of the data included in this publication and accepts no responsibility for any consequence of their use. The mention of specific companies or products of manufacturers does not imply that they are endorsed or recommended by ADB in preference to others of a similar nature that are not mentioned.

By making any designation of or reference to a particular territory or geographic area, or by using the term "country" in this document, ADB does not intend to make any judgments as to the legal or other status of any territory or area.

Corrigenda to ADB publications may be found at http://www.adb.org/publications/corrigenda.

Notes:
In this publication, "$" refers to United States dollars.

Cover design by Michael B. Cortes.

Contents

Boxes

Abbreviations

4IR	Fourth Industrial Revolution
ADB	Asian Development Bank
ASEAN	Association of Southeast Asian Nations
BIMP-EAGA	Brunei Darussalam–Indonesia–Malaysia–Philippines East ASEAN Growth Area
COVID-19	coronavirus disease
GDP	gross domestic product
GHG	greenhouse gas
GMS	Greater Mekong Subregion
GMS-2030	The Greater Mekong Subregion Economic Cooperation Program Strategic Framework 2030
IMT-GT	Indonesia–Malaysia–Thailand Growth Triangle
km	kilometer
Lao PDR	Lao People's Democratic Republic
MSME	micro, small, and medium-sized enterprise
PRC	People's Republic of China
RCI	regional cooperation and integration
RIF	regional investment framework
SDG	Sustainable Development Goal
SEAP	safe and environment-friendly agriculture products
SME	small and medium-sized enterprise
SPS	sanitary and phytosanitary

Executive Summary

The Greater Mekong Subregion (GMS) Economic Cooperation Program Strategic Framework 2030 (GMS-2030) provides a new setting for the development of this subregion for the next decade. It is based on deeper regional cooperation and integration in key areas and builds upon the GMS Program's acknowledged strengths that center on connectivity and a project-led approach to development. GMS-2030 relies on the continued ownership and leadership of its member countries, while aligning itself and adding value to their national development plans. GMS-2030 blends the continuity of approach—based on decades of previously successful strategies, actions plans, and projects—with significant changes in a select number of areas to reflect the current global and regional forces that may impinge on GMS development prospects.

GMS countries are adversely impacted by the coronavirus disease (COVID-19), as are those in the rest of the world, despite their prompt and effective response that initially limited its spread. The GMS, however, is confronted with a deep recession—its most significant challenge in the 28 years since the GMS Program was established. The pandemic is negatively impacting economic growth, incomes, and employment, while threatening the poverty reduction achievements to date that resulted from a combined national effort and successful subregional cooperation. The GMS Program has responded promptly to the pandemic by adding value to national strategies.

GMS-2030 provides a framework for the subregion to act collectively in its response to seven long-term, powerful local trends:

(i) risk of pandemics;

(ii) weaker global growth and the threat to free trade;

(iii) persistent pockets of poverty and increasing in-country inequality;

(iv) severe environmental challenges and threats from climate change, disaster events, and pollution;

(v) technological change and digitalization;

(vi) evolving demographics; and

(vii) rapid urbanization.

The underlying consequences of these for the subregion are grave and have been further exacerbated by the impact of COVID-19. GMS-2030 provides a robust subregional response to these developments, which would be onerous to tackle on an individual country basis.

The GMS-2030 Vision is to develop a more integrated, prosperous, sustainable, and inclusive subregion. To achieve this, GMS-2030 establishes a new Mission Statement with regard to the GMS Program: A subregional cooperation program focused on its fundamental strengths of community, connectivity, and competitiveness while embracing the core principles of environmental sustainability and resilience, internal and external integration, and inclusivity, for building a GMS community with a shared future.

The core principles of GMS-2030 will be infused across all initiatives addressed by the GMS Program. Innovative approaches are also necessary in the following six cross-cutting areas:

(i) **Digital revolution.** Harness the transformative potential of the digital revolution and focus on the preparation of subregional spheres of: (a) digital policies and regulation, (b) internet connectivity, (c) e-commerce and payment systems, (d) in-demand logistics and skills, and (e) risks of using digital technology. GMS-2030 will promote inclusive digitalization and the use of advanced technologies in all GMS Program activities and projects. Focus will be placed on the transport, energy, agriculture, tourism, and health sectors as well as on other areas such as trade, smart cities and micro, small, and medium-sized enterprises (MSMEs), while selectively exploring new areas, such as e-commerce and telecommunications. COVID-19 will likely act as a catalyst in the digital transformation of GMS countries. Digital readiness to date has successfully played a crucial role in some GMS countries in efforts to contain the virus. It also has provided some countries the potential to maintain a relatively open economy during the pandemic.

(ii) **Enhanced spatial approach.** Design an enhanced spatial approach to development that is based on an integrated network of economic corridors, dynamic border areas, and clusters of competitive cities that are well connected to rural areas.

(iii) **Dialogue, knowledge sharing, and capacity building.** Foster deeper dialogue on policies and regulations—underpinned by knowledge-based solutions and improved capacities—to realize the full gains of infrastructure investments and public service delivery. Increased participation of subregional think tanks, universities, and development partners in the GMS Program will be encouraged. Knowledge-sharing events will include policy discussions among GMS countries, with additional countries or subregions. The capacity building of GMS officials will be promoted under an enhanced Brunei Darussalam–Indonesia–Malaysia–Philippines East ASEAN Growth Area (BIMP-EAGA), Indonesia–Malaysia–Thailand Growth Triangle (IMT-GT), and GMS (B-I-G) Capacity Building Program.

(iv) **Private sector solutions.** Embrace private sector solutions to leverage expertise and financing so that they are more relevant post-COVID-19. A spectrum of solutions, private and public, will be considered, and a variety of financing options also explored. GMS public–private forums will be promoted in key sectors and the GMS Business Council will be strengthened.

(v) **GMS as an open platform.** Reform the GMS Program to be a more open platform that cooperates closely with other regional cooperation and integration initiatives, especially the Association of Southeast Asian Nations; Ayeyawady-Chao Phraya-Mekong Economic Cooperation Strategy; the Bay of Bengal Initiative for Multi-Sectoral Technical and Economic Cooperation; the Belt and Road Initiative; the Cambodia-Lao PDR-Myanmar-Viet Nam Cooperation (CLMV); IMT-GT; and the Mekong–Lancang Cooperation.* GMS-2030 also will promote further participation in the GMS Program by local governments, development partners, academia, and civil society to draw from their expertise and financing, especially in relation to new and complex areas.

(vi) **Results framework.** Establish a results framework for monitoring and evaluation.

* The terms Lancang-Mekong Cooperation and Mekong-Lancang Cooperation refer to the same cooperation mechanism and have been used interchangeably in the document.

GMS-2030 will be predicated on three pillars: to build a greater sense of "Community," to achieve increased "Connectivity," and to enhance "Competitiveness." Other areas of cooperation also may be explored under GMS-2030 to ensure that the subregion is able to respond quickly to new challenges, depending on the needs and demands of GMS countries.

Pillar 1: Community. Over the past 28 years, cooperation between GMS countries has yielded fruitful results and deepened a sense of community with a shared future. GMS-2030 will promote the development of a healthy and environmentally sustainable GMS community in which the well-being of all citizens is pursued. The COVID-19 pandemic has placed hygiene, with a clean and safe environment, and effective coordination across national health systems at the center of disease prevention. COVID-19 has highlighted the need to effectively deal with increasingly complex and harmful interactions between humans and wildlife, exacerbated by biodiversity loss and climate change.

- The GMS health agenda will focus on communicable disease control through cross-border surveillance and modeling, information exchange, implementation of international health regulations, and pandemic preparedness. Since universal health coverage is a critical regional public good, GMS-2030 will aim to accelerate its implementation. This will be effected by strengthening the performance of GMS health systems to prevent, detect, and respond to public health threats such as COVID-19 and other emerging diseases; support countries to comply with the World Health Organization's International Health Regulations; apply a unified approach to environmental, animal, and human health ("One Health"); strengthen protection of vulnerable communities and migrants; build capacity and cross-border cooperation to address priority health issues; and advance in gender equality to build subregional health cooperation leadership and decision-making policy.

- GMS-2030 will also focus on improving environmental sustainability and climate change resilience. Environment and climate change challenges will be addressed through green technologies; protection of ecosystems and key ecological processes; climate resilience policies; and disaster-risk management, all of which will recognize the essential role that communities play as stewards of natural resources. A systematic effort will be made to mainstream climate change considerations into all GMS interventions, with a focus on energy efficiency, renewable energy, climate-smart landscapes, and sustainable waste management, particularly in terms of healthy ocean and river systems, and the tackling of plastic pollution.

Pillar 2: Connectivity. GMS-2030 will promote further connectivity within the subregion, as well as the rest of Asia in terms of transport and energy.

- Regarding transport, GMS-2030 will prioritize intermodal approaches, facilitate cross-border transport, and seek improvement in logistics, asset management, and road safety. Given the rise in GMS economic density, and with respect to its environmental considerations, GMS-2030 aims to ensure the development of railway networks; sea, river, and dry ports; and inland waterways. Investments in airports to improve connections with the rest of Asia and the world will be essential, as will the development of secondary roads that will link to main corridors to expand the benefits to poorer communities. An effort will be made to integrate urban transport with the GMS transport network.

- The energy sector will focus on cross-border power trade, establishing regional grid codes, developing regional markets, and expanding clean energy investments with a greater role for the private sector.

Pillar 3: Competitiveness. GMS-2030 will enhance competitiveness post-COVID-19 by restoring and promoting trade and investment facilitation, agriculture, tourism, urban development in a climate-friendly manner and working together to build an open, fair, just and nondiscriminatory business environment.

- The focus on trade facilitation will modernize customs and establish sanitary and phytosanitary regulations. It will also strengthen links to the private sector. GMS-2030 will support the development of e-commerce platforms in the subregion. By facilitating investment, the strategy will ease or eliminate investment flow constraints and create an integrated investment market.

- In the agriculture sector, GMS-2030 will promote higher food safety and quality standards for expanding exports, for which an alignment of policies and standards will be required in the subregion. GMS-2030 also will encourage climate- and environment-friendly production practices along the value chain, as well as sustain natural assets with a focus on small-scale farmers and micro, small, and medium-sized agro-enterprises. Given that COVID-19 has adversely impacted agricultural supply chains, GMS-2030 will support food security response and recovery efforts in the medium and long terms.

- GMS countries have already undertaken various measures to counteract the pandemic's adverse impacts on tourism. These include fiscal, monetary, and training support for the travel and tourism businesses. Since the subregion's tourist industry has been severely impacted, the strategy will promote recovery efforts by developing higher value-added and secondary destinations, as well as strengthen human capital, connectivity infrastructure, public–private linkages, and environmental sustainability.

- The COVID-19 pandemic inevitably will leave its mark on cities, physically and socially, echoing for generations to come. This is already evident in terms of urban life. The GMS Program will focus on these effects with measures to respond to current and future crises. GMS-2030 will encourage a holistic approach to the future planning of cities so that they are green, smart, competitive, resilient, safe, and inclusive. It will also promote linkages between cities to develop new urban clusters and maximize economies of agglomeration, develop cities in border areas, create linkages with special economic and industrial zones, and improve waste management and pollution in cities located close to GMS rivers and seas.

Other areas of cooperation. Taking into consideration the rapid developments, emerging priorities, and multiple challenges that face the subregion, GMS-2030 is designed as a living document that will provide GMS countries and stakeholders alike the flexibility to collaborate in other areas and sectors, as their needs and demands arise.

- As such, the GMS Program will be able to rapidly respond to new challenges and align itself with the United Nations' Sustainable Development Goals. Furthermore, GMS-2030 encourages cooperation in innovative areas such as digitalization and new technologies, e-commerce platforms, logistics, labor mobility and safe migration, education and skills, and special economic zones. In addition, cross-sector collaboration will be promoted.

- Institutional arrangements will be boosted. GMS-2030 will continue to benefit from the well-established, multitiered, institutional mechanisms of the GMS Program, including the triennial Summit of Leaders; annual ministerial conference; and frequent meetings of senior GMS country officials and sector working groups. The institutions that support the GMS Program will remain lean, albeit sufficiently strengthened to respond to the increasingly complex challenges of the next decade. New sector working groups or taskforces will be formed to support the critical areas such as trade and investment facilitation.

- To flexibly cover the new areas and emerging priorities that are included in GMS-2030, the terms of reference of sector working groups will be amended as required and new sector forums will be established to enable the participation of the private sector and knowledge institutions. The Secretariat of the Asian Development Bank will be central to the GMS Program, strengthening its traditional support role. It will be the provider of knowledge, financier, and honest broker and, in close collaboration with national secretariats, will play a more significant role in curating the knowledge, providing a unified public–private response to GMS activities, and nurturing partnerships. The forming of sectoral secretariats and sector meetings at the level of minister will be encouraged for specific sectors. In addition, the GMS Local Governors' Forum and the GMS Business Council will be strengthened.

- Programming and monitoring systems and processes will be enhanced. The Regional Investment Framework will be revised to raise project inclusion standards to increase its appeal to development partners and the private sector with respect to project readiness; economic and social returns; and adherence to environmental and social best practices and project management standards. A GMS Results Framework will monitor GMS-2030.

GMS-2030 seeks to transform the GMS Program into a more strategic mechanism that will support high-level policy dialogue, encourage collaboration, and ensure action. It also aims to harmonize regulatory standards so that infrastructure utilization and the delivery of services are optimized.

I. Rationale for a New Strategic Framework

1. In 1992, Cambodia, the Lao People's Democratic Republic (Lao PDR), Myanmar, the People's Republic of China (PRC) (Guangxi Zhuang Autonomous Region and Yunnan Province), Thailand, and Viet Nam established the Greater Mekong Subregion Economic Cooperation Program (GMS Program or "the Program").[1] A pioneering initiative, the Program has remained resilient, thanks to the strong ownership and commitment of its member countries and the robust leadership from GMS ministers, and officials, as well as the support of the Asian Development Bank (ADB) as the Program's Secretariat. It has pursued a practical, goal-oriented approach and has implemented projects that have concentrated on building infrastructure to foster regional connectivity and integration. The Program has focused on (i) increasing connectivity through the development of physical infrastructure and economic corridors; (ii) improving competitiveness through the facilitation of the cross-border movement of goods, as well as more efficient tourism, agriculture, and urban sectors; and (iii) building a greater sense of community by working together on shared concerns in terms of health and the environment.

2. The Program, to date, has achieved impressive outcomes. Connectivity has been dramatically enhanced by close to 12,000 kilometers (km) of new or upgraded roads and about 700 km of railway lines. Nearly 3,000 megawatts of electricity has been generated, and over 2,600 km of transmission and distribution lines now provide electricity access to about 150,000 new households. The subregion's competitiveness has been

Climate change and natural disasters. (above) The region is vulnerable to impacts of climate change and natural disasters, including intense drought and precipitation, recurrent flooding, and rising sea levels.

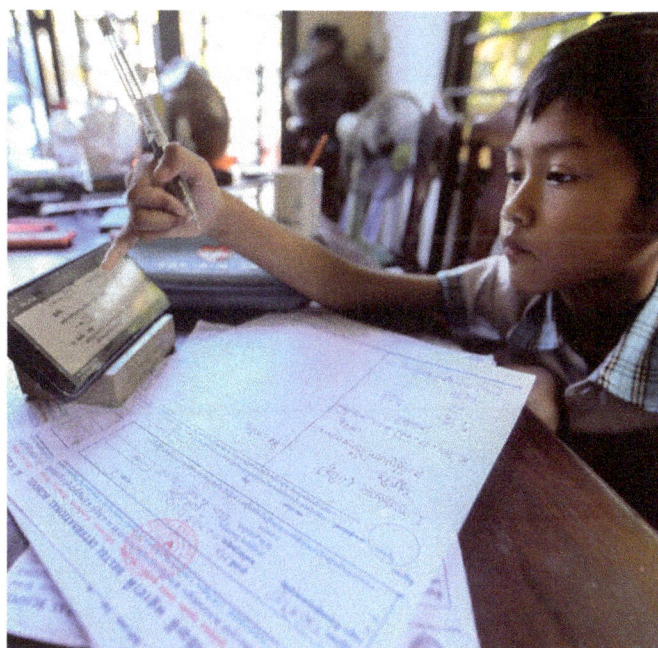

COVID-19 and other pandemic threats. (right) The COVID-19 pandemic has resulted in schools being shut all over the world. As a result, distance learning using digital platforms has become the norm.

---

[1] The Guangxi Zhuang Autonomous Region of the PRC joined the GMS Program in 2004.

Rapid urbanization. The number of people living in cities of the Greater Mekong Subregion is increasing fast. Traffic congestion has become a normal occurrence in many major cities.

strengthened by the Program's efforts to facilitate transport and trade flows, strengthen agriculture, develop urban areas, and promote the GMS as a single tourist destination. Trade between GMS countries has grown from $25.6 billion in 2000 to $639.4 billion in 2020. Foreign direct investment into the GMS has averaged $26.9 billion a year between 2010 and 2019. Close to 80 million international tourists visited the GMS in 2019, generating receipts of $101 billion.[2] The Program has reduced travel cost and time, as well as increased the movement of goods and people across land routes in the subregion, improved agriculture productivity, and created additional jobs. Furthermore, it has advanced community building through initiatives to check the spread of communicable diseases, protect the subregion's rich biodiversity, and mitigate the impacts of climate change. The Program has improved natural resource management of 2.6 million hectares in seven transboundary landscapes.

3.   The GMS Program, since 1992, has mobilized $27.7 billion in financing (45% contributed by ADB, 22% by GMS governments, and 33% by development partners and the private sector) to support 109 cross-cutting investment and 230 technical assistance projects. The Program has well-established and lean institutional arrangements, including the triennial Summit of Leaders, annual ministerial conference, sector working groups, economic corridor forums, and local governors' forums.[3] These arrangements allow the members of the GMS to collectively determine Program priorities; agree on regional investments, knowledge creation and sharing, and technical assistance; and seek funding for its activities from international and bilateral financial institutions, as well as from private sector sources, to complement their own investments. The GMS Program also has clear planning and programming arrangements. The first strategic framework for the Program was endorsed by GMS leaders in 2002[4] and a second one was approved in 2012.[5] GMS leaders approved the Ha Noi Action Plan in March 2018 to accelerate Program implementation.[6] The GMS Regional Investment Framework (RIF) provides a list of priority projects that is reviewed and updated annually.

4.   The coronavirus disease (COVID-19) has transformed the GMS and the world. The subregion now faces its deepest recession in decades and the GMS Program is confronted with its most significant challenge in its 28 years of existence. The pandemic may lead to a long-term contraction of growth, income, and employment.

---

[2]   Data from the Mekong Tourism Coordinating Office, Guangxi Zhuang Autonomous Region, and Yunnan Province are not available.
[3]   So far, each GMS member has hosted a Summit of Leaders. The 7th summit will be held in Cambodia in 2021.
[4]   ADB. 2002. The Strategic Framework for the Next Ten Years of the Greater Mekong Subregion Economic Cooperation Program. Manila. https://www.adb.org/publications/strategic-framework-ten-years-gms-economic-cooperation-program.
[5]   ADB. 2011. The Greater Mekong Subregion Economic Cooperation Program Strategic Framework 2012–2022. Manila. www.adb.org/sites/default/files/institutional-document/33422/files/gms-ec-framework-2012-2022.pdf.
[6]   ADB. 2018. The Ha Noi Action Plan 2018–2022. Manila. www.adb.org/sites/default/files/institutional-document/409086/ha-noi-action-plan-2018-2022.pdf.

This, in turn, could negatively impact a decade of progress on poverty reduction won through rising subregional cooperation across a range of activities, particularly trade and connectivity. The GMS Program has demonstrated its usefulness and responded quickly and effectively to the pandemic, adding value to national strategies (Box 1). The effective reaction of GMS countries to the pandemic has kept the number of people affected and the number of deaths due to COVID-19 at very low levels compared with other subregions around the globe. GMS economies, businesses, and households, however, are severely affected and many vulnerable people are suffering. Some of the changes produced by the pandemic, however, have the potential of permanent and more structural implications for the subregion, thus demanding a longer-term collaboration of GMS countries. The GMS Economic Cooperation Program Strategic Framework 2030 (GMS-2030) aims to provide a holistic response to existing and new challenges. It will focus on the long-term implications for GMS economies through 2030, taking into account medium-term priorities.

5.   In light of the economic shock brought about by COVID-19, GMS-2030 will prioritize subregional cooperation in pandemic management and, in the medium term, will focus on supporting a steady recovery from the pandemic. GMS-2030 will strengthen GMS activities and make subregional cooperation more robust, such that it will be better able to deal with external vulnerabilities (i.e., growth, trade, climate change, and the impact of technology) while also better managing internal factors such as demographics, urbanization, and inequality. Under GMS-2030, GMS countries also commit to increase coordination in their macroeconomic policies to counteract the negative impacts of the crisis and to work together to ensure industrial and supply chains remain stable.

6.   As regional cooperation initiatives in the region continue to grow, the GMS Program must be able to adapt to changing circumstances in order to remain relevant and effective, while expanding collaboration with other regional cooperation and integration (RCI) initiatives. Moreover, the Program has to proactively identify the new imperatives in the development agenda, such as innovation and technology, digitalization, the changing nature of work, and the manifold impact of climate so as to maximize the gains from regional cooperation.

Box 1:   Greater Mekong Subregion Program's COVID-19 Response

The coronavirus disease (COVID-19) continues to have profound health and economic impacts across the Greater Mekong Subregion (GMS), with subregional gross domestic product growth contracted at 0.2% in 2020 compared to 2019 (5.4%). The pandemic has also highlighted the effectiveness of GMS cooperation to provide an immediate response in critical sectors. The GMS Program (the Program), through its project-oriented approach, is responding with immediate assistance to strengthen resilience and economic recovery in several areas, including health, transport and trade facilitation, agriculture and food security, tourism management, and urban development.

Health cooperation. The Program has enabled a rapid response to COVID-19 including (i) assistance in the procurement of diagnostic and laboratory equipment to combat the outbreak; (ii) policy dialogue to strengthen regional collaboration and address common capacity constraints hampering the effective response to COVID-19 at regional and country levels alike; and (iii) strengthening public health security mechanisms, including surveillance and outbreak responses, laboratory quality and biosafety, and access to health services. The Program has supported delivery of thermal scanners, personal protective equipment, real-time polymerase chain reaction machines, infrared thermometers, laboratory equipment, and intensive care unit respiratory ventilators.

Transport and trade facilitation. COVID-19 is affecting supply chains across the globe. The Program currently supports GMS countries to strengthen resilience for the future by accelerating the implementation of the GMS road transport permit, electronic customs clearance, and digital tracking through technologies such as

continued next page

Box 1 *continued*

blockchain, on-board mass, and radio frequency identification. Investments and common standards in border crossing infrastructure will now include health screening and further improvements in customs, immigration, quarantine, and security to ensure trade flows and supply chains continue to move smoothly in the subregion.

Agriculture and food security. The Program is assisting GMS countries to ensure food security and environmental sustainability as a critical component of GMS countries' response to COVID-19. The GMS Working Group on Agriculture organized a virtual dialogue on "Priorities for Post-Pandemic Food Security and Response and Recovery in the GMS," and has initiated work on "Digital Technologies for Greening Agribusiness Supply Chains and Accelerating Post-Pandemic Recovery" in the GMS and on "Priorities for Post-Pandemic Livestock Health and Value Chains Improvement in the GMS." The Program will organize a special session on "Priorities for Food Safety Risk Communication" in the context of COVID-19 to take this work forward.

Tourism management. The pandemic has significantly impacted the tourism sector in the subregion and threatens to reverse strikingly successful tourism service exports in the GMS, that have recorded high annual growth in recent years exceeding global and Asian averages. Tourism in 2019 contributed from 4.6% to 26.4% of GMS countries' gross domestic product and employed millions of workers. GMS countries, with the support of the Program, have effectively responded to the COVID-19 pandemic, implementing the following measures to protect public health and keep the tourism industry afloat: the tourism industry (i) provided clear travel advisories and widely disseminated accurate information about travel regulations; (ii) ensured fiscal, monetary, and training support for a broad range of travel and tourism enterprises, including micro, small, and medium-sized businesses; (iii) implemented social protection programs to safeguard formal and informal workers' income and livelihoods; (iv) developed health and safety regulations for key tourism subsectors; (v) provided monetary incentives to energize domestic tourism ahead of reopening to international visitors; and (vi) prepared and began implementing tourism recovery plans. The impact mitigation initiatives and projects, led by the GMS Tourism Working Group and the Mekong Tourism Coordinating Office included (i) the creation of a COVID-19 resource webpage on each country, including travel restrictions, and another on policy updates for each; (ii) dissemination of infographic sheets to provide a quick overview of the situation in each member country; (iii) establishment of the Mekong Memories initiative, where travel businesses in the region will be able to reach out to their past clients and encourage them to share their experiences, thus motivating people to visit the subregion when travel resumes; (iv) creation of the Mekong Deals webpage that showcases nonrefundable vouchers and gift certificates offered by tourism businesses in the region as cash relief measures; (v) provision of flexible capacity-building activities to respond to post-COVID-19 needs, such as developing or implementing safety protocols and standards; and (vi) ensuring improved market access for tourists in the subregion.

Urban development. In urban development, the Program's response has focused on the (i) provision of essential water, sanitation, and hygiene services by enhancing water and sanitation facilities in urban operations, ranging from hand washing stations in public spaces to the provision of water supply in urban areas with high population density and nonexistent basic infrastructure; (ii) smooth delivery of essential utility services—that is, providing financial and technical support to utilities struggling with a loss of revenue, reduced availability of critical materials, and deferred investments; (iii) provision of public transport and response to the changing travel needs of citizens during COVID-19 by enhancing social distancing measures, fleet sanitation, enforcement of safety protocols in informal modes of transport, and management of commuters' expectations; and (iv) reuse of public spaces to help communities maintain distance during COVID-19, as well as remodel available spaces in commercial, office, and industrial buildings.

Source: ADB GMS Secretariat.

A.   Changing Subregion

7.   While COVID-19 has transformed the GMS, the challenges and opportunities that the subregion and the GMS Program will face in the following decade include other important, complex, and often interconnected areas. Seven powerful trends affect the global and regional environment with lasting implications for GMS countries and the GMS Program.

1.   COVID-19 and Other Pandemic Threats

8.   Global and regional pandemic threats are well recognized in the GMS, including the transmission of emerging, reemerging, and epidemic-prone diseases. The spread of cross-border diseases has serious consequences on GMS economies given that they are connected by land and maritime borders that are crossed by many workers daily. The COVID-19 pandemic is a powerful reminder of our interconnectedness. Combating this pandemic calls for collective action in the spirit of solidarity.

9.   The legacy of the pandemic will be particularly pronounced in health care systems and the heightened need for regional cooperation in health information and health services. In addition to strengthened clinical care systems, pandemic preparedness will require additional spending in areas such as virus and antibody testing, building contact tracer systems, and developing an inventory of personal protective equipment. Regional cooperation will be of particular importance in strengthening systems for transparent and rapid information sharing, as well as for fostering open trade in equipment, medical services, and vaccines.

10.   Cross-border and subregional cooperation must be strengthened to maximize synergies and partnerships between and among the health systems of GMS countries, consolidating health security as a regional public good that carries benefits for people across the subregion. The GMS will need to build scenarios that will take risk factors explicitly into account and develop mechanisms to respond with speed and flexibility as risks arise.

11.   GMS countries will have to commit to take all necessary measures to fight this pandemic, protect lives, safeguard people's jobs and income, minimize disruptions to trade and supply chains in the subregion, and introduce supportive policies to help small and medium-sized enterprises (SMEs) tide over the difficulties. This will include border areas where there can be pronounced health impacts and where, often, the network of appropriate health and social services is weak. Socioeconomic inequalities increase vulnerability to disease outbreaks.

2.   Weaker Global Growth and Threats to Free Trade

12.   Global gross domestic product (GDP) contracted to unprecedented levels in 2020 with every region in the world in recession. Mitigating measures taken by countries to reduce infection constrained output while uncertainty brought about by the COVID-19 pandemic limited demand. In Asia, slowing growth was already taking place even before the COVID-19 shock because of global trade conflicts. Consistent with other parts of the world, GDP growth in the GMS slowed down in 2020 (0.2%) compared to 2019 (5.4%). While GDP growth is expected to recover in 2021 (4.5%), the medium-term outlook for growth in GMS remains subdued given broad declines in consumption, investment, and trade (especially tourism). Country performance will vary depending on countries' access to the COVID-19 vaccine, effectiveness of government policy response, and individual structural characteristics of countries.

13.   GMS members are likely to be deeply affected by the disruption of supply chains since most of their economies are integrated with international and regional value chains. GMS growth has relied on expanding trade, exploiting cost advantages in manufacturing and services, and realizing productivity gains from foreign direct investment. Escalating trade tensions threaten this growth model, with sustained pressures undermining

confidence—especially in financial markets—disrupting supply chains, and discouraging investments. Even before the onset of the pandemic, it was estimated that protectionist pressures could lead to a drop in Asian GDP by 0.9% over the next 2 years and tighter global financial conditions by a further 0.75% of GDP.[7] The long-term blow to the supply side of economies cannot be quantified as yet;[8] however, with the destruction of part of the capital stock and erosion of labor skills, falling labor participation, breaking of supply chains, and possible enduring effects on international trade, the blow could be significant. Business costs are expected to rise as workplace safety regulations are tightened through new workplace norms that relate to the proximity of COVID-19 safety equipment for workers on the work floor or in production lines. In addition, investments will have to be made to enhance production resilience, such as to ensure shorter and more local supply chains, which will prove costlier; and facilitate greater inventories, which will affect productivity and costs and have long-term growth impacts.

14.   Annual growth is projected to be subdued from 2020–2025 in Asia's emerging and developing countries.[9] Over the medium term (2021–2022), risks to the outlook remain on the downside, as evidenced by waves of COVID-19 infections that could persist well into 2022 and new variants of the virus that are emerging.[10] Lower economic activity may trigger external debt defaults, a drying-up of capital inflows, and a weakening of banking systems. Further risks include unresolved international trade tensions, high oil price volatility, and widespread social unrest from falling incomes.

15.   Over the long term (2023–2030), growth in the GMS will be affected by the weakening of the supply side of economies from several factors. A part of the capital stock will be rendered obsolete through the destruction of supply chains. Insolvencies will remove capital from production. Moreover, productivity growth may be permanently affected. Skills in the labor supply may deteriorate if unemployment persists. Despite these adverse forces, GMS economies could experience a reversion to high rates of sustained growth over the long term if the pandemic subsides (or if the policy response in containing the pandemic is effective including wide and equitable administration of COVID-19 vaccines) and if economic and development policies are reoriented toward strengthening human capital, adopting digital technologies, and enhancing productivity.

3.   Persistent Pockets of Poverty and In-Country Inequality

16.   Since the creation of the GMS Program in 1992, the subregion has experienced rapid growth in incomes, leading to a sharp fall in poverty in all GMS countries. Rapid growth and better-targeted social policies have also contributed to reduced inequalities within some of the GMS countries, although high in-country inequality is still persistent across the GMS. Inequality between GMS countries also persists, despite some progress on per capita income convergence.

17.   Although poverty has shrunk markedly in the subregion, there remain persistent pockets of poverty, especially in remote rural or mountainous areas and in border communities. Such areas face a disadvantage in access to, participation in, and benefit from public services such as health care, financial services and markets, clean energy, and water and sanitation.[11] In-country inequalities have escalated in recent years in some GMS countries, driven by

[7]   International Monetary Fund. 2018. *Regional Economic Outlook. Asia Pacific: Good Times, Uncertain Times: A Time to Prepare. World Economic and Financial Surveys.* Washington, DC. www.imf.org/en/Publications/REO/APAC/Issues/2018/04/16/areo0509.

[8]   The scarring effect on the supply potential of economies depends on the still uncertain duration and intensity of the worldwide second wave of infections, as well as the speed and coverage of the delivery of vaccines at a late stage of development.

[9]   International Monetary Fund. 2020. World Economic Outlook, October 2020. Washington, DC. GDP in emerging and developing Asia is projected to contract by 1.7% in 2020, but forecast to grow by an annual average of 6.5% over 2021–2025. https://www.imf.org/external/datamapper/NGDP_RPCH@WEO/OEMDC/ADVEC/WEOWORLD/DA (accessed November 2020).

[10]   Statement by WHO Special Envoy on COVID-19. https://www.solothurnerzeitung.ch/wirtschaft/corona-sondergesandter-besorgt-in-der-schweiz-koennte-ein-sehr-hohes-niveau-von-erkrankungen-und-todesfaellen-erreicht-werden-139939164.

[11]   United Nations Economic and Social Commission for Asia and the Pacific (UNESCAP). 2018. *Inequality in Asia and the Pacific in the Era of 2030 Agenda for Sustainable Development.* www.unescap.org/sites/default/files/publications/ThemeStudyOnInequality.pdf.

technology and uneven human capital accumulation that exacerbates the effects of geographic location, access to public services, and household composition.[12]

18.   Disparities also are evident in gender gaps in productivity, opportunity, wages, and income poverty, particularly in households headed by women. Countries in the subregion boast high adolescent fertility rates[13] and low wage equity.[14] Such developments could undermine social cohesion, endanger social stability, and hamper the subregion's economic prospects.[15] The highly adverse social impacts of the pandemic on gender inequality and opportunities for work, migration, and access to services affect all GMS countries and it will be necessary to protect and enhance women's job and income prospects by acknowledging their roles in the informal and formal sectors, upgrading their skills, and supporting programs that enable them to take advantage of the new challenges and changing opportunities created in the subregion by the crisis.

19.   The pandemic threatens to reverse some hard-won gains in poverty reduction in the subregion. The unequal impact of COVID-19 on some sectors and jobs will continue to expose the poor and vulnerable to greater risks of unemployment, financial losses, and health hazards, exacerbating socioeconomic inequalities and undermining inclusive growth efforts. The steep decline in activity due to the pandemic has resulted in increased unemployment. The market for low-skilled workers and the informal economy have been particularly affected, largely because of the disproportionate impact of the pandemic on the services sector, particularly hospitality, and reduced demand for small trading and manufacturing enterprises. The impact on high-wage employment, given the use of technology and the option of working from home, is less pronounced. Furthermore, income losses appear to have been uneven, with women among the lower-income groups shouldering losses in employment and income. Similarly, the impact on the demand for migrant labor in the GMS has been severe.[16] Additionally, there are pronounced health impacts on border areas where large migrant populations reside or transit through. Labor effects have also highlighted the digital divide within the populations in the subregion with long-term implications for policy and regional cooperation.

20.   In the next decade, it will be critical to attack residual pockets of poverty and reduce income inequality with policies that encourage sustainable urbanization, ensure equal access to public goods and services, strengthen social protection systems, develop subregional and national mechanisms to protect vulnerable populations from the potential negative effects of globalization, and strengthen governance and the quality of institutions. More equitable and inclusive human capital development could, furthermore, boost economic growth, prosperity, and sustainability for the subregion.[17]

---

[12]   The gap in education leads to diminished prospects for employment for the less-educated workers. Female-headed households are less educated and are viewed as having inferior personal characteristics (e.g., age, marital status), resulting in a lower propensity to be employed. ADBI. 2019. *Demystifying Rising Inequality in Asia*. www.adb.org/sites/default/files/publication/485186/adbi-demystifying-rising-inequality-asia.pdf.

[13]   2018 data (births per 1,000 women ages 15–19): Cambodia (50.7), Lao PDR (64.9), Myanmar (28.2), Thailand (44.7), and Viet Nam (29.2) compared to the global average of 42.0. World Bank. Gender Data Portal. https://databank.worldbank.org/id/2ddc971b?Code=SP.ADO. TFRT&report_name=Gender_Indicators_Report&populartype=series.

[14]   Equal pay for work of equal value.

[15]   The United Nations estimates that the Asia and Pacific region could have lifted around 153 million more people out of poverty if income inequality had not increased in 10 countries (Bangladesh, India, Indonesia, the Lao PDR, the PRC, the Republic of Korea, Singapore, Sri Lanka, Tajikistan, and Viet Nam) during the past decade. UNESCAP. 2018. Inequality in Asia and the Pacific in the Era of 2030 Agenda for Sustainable Development. United Nations. www.unescap.org/sites/default/files/publications/ThemeStudyOnInequality.pdf.

[16]   Of the approximately 2 billion informally employed workers worldwide, the International Labour Organization estimates that close to 80% have been significantly affected. IMF. 2020. A Crisis Like No Other, An Uncertain Recovery. *World Economic Outlook Update. June 2020.* www.imf.org/en/Publications/WEO/Issues/2020/06/24/WEOUpdateJune2020.

[17]   McKinsey Global Institute. 2018. *The Power of Parity: Advancing Women's Equality in Asia and the Pacific.* https://www.mckinsey.com/featured-insights/gender-equality/the-power-of-parity-advancing-womens-equality-in-asia-pacific.

4.   Severe Environmental Challenges and Threats from Climate Change, Disaster Events, and Pollution

21.   The impact of COVID-19 is likely to further aggravate the subregion's vulnerability to climate change and disaster events, including long and intense periods of drought, intense precipitation in short periods, recurrent flooding, greater variability in rainfall and temperatures, rising sea levels, degradation of terrestrial and aquatic ecosystems, increasing levels of salinity along coastal regions due to storm surges, and contamination of aquifers from saline water intrusion.[18] The subregion also suffers from air, land, and water pollution. The top polluters represent a small number of large enterprises (e.g., textile, cement, lime, and plaster sectors) concentrated in urban fringes, economic and industrial zones, and near major transport and trade infrastructure and high population density.[19] In the last 30 years, the subregion has lost approximately 30% of its forest cover due to population growth, land use change, and certain policies that prioritize short-term economic growth, among others. Deforestation has had a direct negative impact on wildlife due to habitat loss and the disruption of usual migratory routes.[20] Accelerating biodiversity loss, coupled with drastic changes in land use, will bring wildlife, livestock, and humans into closer contact with each other and could facilitate the spread of diseases, including new strains of bacteria and viruses. Likewise, the increased illegal and uncontrolled trade in live wild animals in the subregion creates dangerous opportunities for contact between humans and the diseases these creatures carry. In addition, plastic pollution is a growing concern, whereby the Mekong River has been identified as one of the 10 rivers that transports 88%–95% of the global load of plastics into the sea.[21]

22.   GMS countries could suffer a huge loss in GDP by 2030, due to inefficient agriculture, fishing, and tourism methods, together with a significant degradation in human health and labor productivity (footnote 18). Myanmar, Thailand, and Viet Nam are among the 10 countries that have been most vulnerable to the impact of extreme weather events in the past 20 years.[22] The subregion faces particularly high exposure to flood hazards, with Viet Nam ranked first (jointly with Bangladesh) globally, accounting for 97% of average annual loss from hazards equating to approximately $2.3 billion. Average annual loss from natural hazards in Cambodia and the Lao PDR is between 1% and 2% of GDP, largely attributable to flooding.[23] In Cambodia, 4 million people, or 25% of the population, are affected every time an extreme river flood strikes.[24] Countries in the subregion have varying levels of capacity to reduce current and future risks from climate change and disasters and to manage the residual risk through improved preparedness, thereby strengthening overall resilience. Greater emphasis on collaborative and participatory action is needed.

23.   GMS cities also contribute to climate change and increased pollution of regional public goods, such as rivers and seas, with many of the biggest urban areas situated along riverbanks or coastal areas. The loss of rivers, lakes, and ocean ecosystems from degradation, overexploitation, and pollution is another important threat to the GMS,

---

[18]   Y. E. Hijioka et al. 2014. Asia. In *Climate Change 2014: Impacts, Adaptation, and Vulnerability. Part B: Regional Aspects. Contribution of Working Group II to the Fifth Assessment Report of the Intergovernmental Panel on Climate Change* [Barros, V.R., C.B. Field, D.J. Dokken, M.D. Mastrandrea, K.J. Mach, T.E. Bilir, M. Chatterjee, K.L. Ebi,Y.O. Estrada, R.C. Genova, B. Girma, E.S. Kissel, A.N. Levy, S. MacCracken, P.R. Mastrandrea, and L.L. White (eds.)]. pp. 1327–1370. Cambridge University Press, Cambridge, United Kingdom and New York, NY.

[19]   ADB. 2018. *Projecting Industrial Pollution in the Greater Mekong Subregion*. Greater Mekong Subregion Core Environment Program. GMS Environment Operations Center. Bangkok. www.adb.org/sites/default/files/publication/435341/projecting-industrial-pollution-gms.pdf.

[20]   World Wide Fund for Nature. 2019. Challenges: Deforestation. http://greatermekong.panda.org/challenges_in_the_greater_mekong/deforestation.

[21]   Schmidt, C., T. Krauth, and S. Wagner. 2017. Export of Plastic Debris by Rivers into the Sea. *Environmental Science & Technology*. 51(21): 12246–12253. www.gwern.net/docs/economics/2017-schmidt.pdf.

[22]   Kreft, S., D. Eckstein, and I. Melchior. 2016. Global Climate Risk Index 2017: Who Suffers Most from Extreme Weather Events? Weather Related Loss Events in 2015 and 1996 to 2015. *Germanwatch Briefing Paper*. Bonn: Germanwatch. https://germanwatch.org/sites/germanwatch.org/files/publication/16411.pdf.

[23]   United Nations Office for Disaster Risk Reduction. 2014. PreventionWeb: Basic Country Statistics and indicators. www.preventionweb.net/countries.

[24]   Willner, S., A. Levermann, F. Zhao, and K. Frieler. 2018. Adaptation Required to Preserve Future High-End River Flood Risk at Present Levels. *Science Advances*. 4(1). https://advances.sciencemag.org/content/4/1/eaao1914.

given the importance of coastal tourism and fisheries for the economy and livelihoods, and the role that coastal ecosystems play as natural buffers for the coastline.

5.   Technological Change and Digitalization

24.   Asia has reaped impressive gains through digitalization.[25] Some GMS countries, however, have lagged, largely because of policy and regulatory constraints, limited skills, and inadequate infrastructure. These countries are well behind advanced Asia as measured by internet access and penetration, internet speed, and new services relating to cloud computing or the Internet of Things, as well as in digital technologies based on artificial intelligence or robotics.

25.   COVID-19 has exposed the impact of the digital divide on the ability to work and seize related opportunities; on the patterns of commerce and trade; and on citizens' access to government services and payments. For a sustained and inclusive recovery, investing in digital infrastructure shaping policies and regulations to help the private sector digitalize, improving people's access to government and payment services, and expanding e-commerce will be critical. The Fourth Industrial Revolution (4IR) represents a clustering of disruptive technologies[26] that requires investments in digital infrastructure and skills.[27] Opportunities for the GMS are immense at the subregional level, especially as global and regional high-tech value chain linkages can be now harnessed.[28] Recovery and achievement of productivity gains at the subregional level will depend on information flows, trade links, investment, and financial service links. To realize productivity gains, new economic and human capital activities in new forms of manufacturing, education, health, and financial services need to be generated. Moreover, leapfrogging opportunities must be created, given the absence of heavy legacy investments. Significantly, micro, small, and medium-sized enterprises (MSMEs) benefit disproportionately by the creation of microtransactions.

26.   In the GMS, digitalization, backed by artificial intelligence, has the potential to transform trade facilitation; increase the feasibility of local and renewable energy production; improve the connectivity of remote areas; and raise standards in agriculture production, education, and health services. Artificial intelligence could accelerate the rate of innovation and employee productivity improvements.[29] Digitalization could also improve domestic resource mobilization. At the same time, the productivity gains via the augmentation of human capacities or automation could impact heavily on the labor market, as well as the education and training sector. The latter will have to adapt to the emerging requirements of employers, as well as the need for entrepreneurship skills that can compensate for the lack of salaried jobs. GMS countries will have to cooperate to maximize the huge opportunities offered by technological progress, while preparing to minimize the risks and accommodate any potential negative impacts.

---

[25]   International Monetary Fund. 2018. Asia's Digital Revolution. *Finance & Development.* September. 55(3). www.imf.org/external/pubs/ft/fandd/2018/09/asia-digital-revolution-sedik.htm.

[26]   Disruptive technologies are generally considered to encompass artificial intelligence, robotics, the Internet of Things, 3D printing, electric vehicles and battery technology, big data applications, and highly customized manufacturing, as well as ledger-based technologies (blockchain settlement) and logistics technologies.

[27]   Philbeck, T., and N. Davis. 2019. The Fourth Industrial Revolution: Shaping a New Era. *Journal of International Affairs.* 22 January. Columbia/ School of International and Public Affairs. https://jia.sipa.columbia.edu/fourth-industrial-revolution-shaping-new-era.

[28]   The GMS, albeit not an early starter, will be able to benefit from the more rapid diffusion in new technologies being made possible by globalization and digitalization. Perkins, R. and E. Neumayer. 2005. The International Diffusion of New Technologies: A Multitechnology Analysis of Latecomer Advantage and Global Economic Integration. *LSE Research Online.* London. https://core.ac.uk/download/pdf/92712.pdf; and McGrath, R. Gunther. 2013. The Pace of Technology Adoption Is Speeding Up. *Harvard Business Review.* 25 November (updated 25 September 2019). https://hbr.org/2013/11/the-pace-of-technology-adoption-is-speeding-up.5.

[29]   Microsoft and IDC Asia/Pacific. 2019. Microsoft–IDC Study: Artificial Intelligence to Nearly Double the Rate of Innovation in Asia Pacific by 2021. Stories from Asia. 20 February. Microsoft. https://news.microsoft.com/apac/2019/02/20/microsoft-idc-study-artificial-intelligence-to-nearly-double-the-rate-of-innovation-in-asia-pacific-by-2021/.

27.   Distance activities (e.g., work, commerce, or the delivery of services and information) are greatly facilitated by sound digital infrastructure and systems, as well as access to them. Over the long term, the nature of commercial transactions, facilitated by digital payment systems—and indeed the nature of work—is likely to change, given the experiences of the COVID-19 pandemic and the need to build greater economic resilience. There are clear implications for skills development and for training the work force of tomorrow. The sharp rise in the share of not only commerce but also of government services (including payments) delivered through digital means illuminates the potential for the future, just as it indicates the need to broaden access to e-government. GMS cooperation over digital policies will be critical to maximize the impact on productivity and growth.[30]

6.   Evolving Demographics

28.   The conjunction of rapid technological development, more gender equality,[31] and aging in certain GMS countries[32] (i.e., the PRC, Thailand, and Viet Nam) amplifies the disruptions to labor markets, the changing demand for skills,[33] and the need for more efficient and inclusive human resource practices through subregional collaboration. Thailand and Viet Nam are expected to complete the transition from aging to aged societies—with between 14% and 20% of the population 60 years or older—in 2024 and 2039, respectively, while a quarter of the PRC's population is expected to age over 60 by 2030. Increasing aging populations in these countries will significantly increase health and social security costs, as well as place pressures on government budgets and social protection systems.

29.   At the same time, other GMS countries will enjoy the demographic dividend from a youthful workforce, although it will need to create jobs for them. The 4IR—coupled with the medium- to long-term impact of the pandemic—will, as noted, transform the nature of manufacturing, thus eroding the competitive edge of low-cost, low-skilled labor in manufacturing on which some of the GMS countries have relied for their past growth. This change demands an upskilling of the existing workforce and greater labor mobility to realize gains from improving efficiency in the allocation of labor. The GMS will need to develop mechanisms to facilitate labor migration of both skilled and unskilled labor in a secure manner from GMS countries with young populations to those countries within and beyond GMS with rapidly aging populations. Migration policies will need to reflect population shifts induced by climate change. These policies should be based on greater integration within and outside the GMS, as well as a greater equity in access for migrants in education and health services, agriculture, energy, and transport in order to maximize gains.

7.   Rapid Urbanization

30.   The COVID-19 crisis has disproportionately impacted cities, since they are densely populated and more exposed to connections. The crisis also presents opportunities for cities, since evidence has shown that their air

---

[30]   Discussed in detail in Section III-A of this report.

[31]   All countries in the region have recorded higher male labor force participation rates, with Myanmar having experienced the widest differential rate of 51.7% female compared to 81.5% male labor participation; and the Lao PDR having reported the closest alignment, with a rate of 80.7% female participation compared to 82.2% male. World Economic Forum. 2019. Global Gender Gap Report 2020. Insight Report. Geneva. www3.weforum.org/docs/WEF_GGGR_2020.pdf.

[32]   The old-age dependency ratio (the ratio of over 65 years old to working age population) is projected to rise in the PRC from 13.1% in 2015 to 25.3% in 2030 and to 46.7% in 2050; corresponding figures for Thailand are 14.6%, 29.2%, and 52.5%, respectively; with the projected rise in Viet Nam being much more modest, at 9.6%, 18.3%, and 34.1%, respectively. International Monetary Fund. 2017. *Regional Economic Outlook. Asia and Pacific: Preparing for Choppy Seas*. World Economic and Financial Surveys. Washington, DC. www.imf.org/en/Publications/REO/APAC/Issues/2017/04/28/areo0517.

[33]   ADB. 2019. *Skilled Labor Mobility and Migration: Challenges and Opportunities for the ASEAN Economic Community*. Manila. www.adb.org/sites/default/files/publication/517601/skilled-labor-mobility-migration-asean.pdf.

quality has improved around the world as economic activity has slowed, vehicle traffic has fallen, and more people work from home.[34] This also has led to a potentially direct and measurable impact on public health in cities.[35]

31.   The GMS is one of the least urbanized subregions in the world, with relatively low urbanization levels that range from 19.5% in Cambodia to 44.2% in Thailand. The number of people living in cities in the subregion, however, is increasing fast. The urbanization growth rates of all GMS countries are higher than the world average, ranging from 4.9% annually in Yunnan Province in the PRC, to a low of 2.6% annually in Myanmar.[36] It is estimated that by 2030, more than 40% of the GMS population will be living in cities.

32.   Despite low urbanization generally in all GMS countries, urban areas account for a much larger percentage of GDP—at least half in most countries and approximately 75% in Thailand—than the share of its national populations. In Thailand, urban GDP is characterized by a solid middle-income standard of living, followed by the PRC's Guangxi Zhuang Autonomous Region and Yunnan Province. Increasingly, cities and towns in the GMS are becoming engines of economic growth and centers of culture and innovation. They now account for approximately 50%–60% of the subregion's economic production and, by 2050—when urban areas in the GMS reach 64%–74% of the population—urban GDP will grow to an estimated 70%–80% (footnote 36).

33.   Urbanization forms a pivotal part of the subregion's rapid shift from predominantly agriculture to manufacturing, services, and knowledge-driven economies. These developments raise several issues related to transport, water supply, infrastructure, waste management, sanitation, environmental sustainability, equity of opportunity, poverty, and shelter, and require a new framework for urban development. GMS cities are also becoming one of the greatest contributors to climate change and the increased pollution of regional public goods, such as rivers and seas, with many of the biggest urban areas situated along riverbanks or coastal areas. The main challenges for the subregion therefore are to deal with the implications of rapid urbanization; that is, to make cities more livable, to cooperate among cities to reduce the negative impacts on regional public goods, and to develop clusters of cities that become the engines of GMS growth.

34.   Post-COVID-19, urban planning in the GMS should promote a more holistic approach to city planning by combining grey, green, and blue infrastructure. This approach will support the strategies that aim to achieve not only a better public health response, but also overall disaster and climate change resilience. New planning approaches must include open spaces, watersheds, forests, and parks into the heart of how to think about cities. Strengthening and supporting regional and corridor cooperation will lead to more integrated city-regional planning around economies, energy provision, transportation, and food production. As a result, these networks have the potential to become pillars of resilience rather than sources of high vulnerability. A greater focus on housing must be ensured, including the upgrade of informal settlements and improved access to affordable housing and public space. In addition, non-motorized forms of transport, such as walking and cycling, should be promoted.

---

[34]   However, these effects have been shown to be temporary as cities move out of lockdowns.
[35]   Dixon, T. 2020. What Impacts Are Emerging from Covid-19 for Urban Futures? 8 June. *The Centre for Evidence-Based Medicine.* https://www.cebm.net/covid-19/what-impacts-are-emerging-from-covid-19-for-urban-futures/.
[36]   For more information, see Greater Mekong Subregion: Rural No More. 2017 (updated). www.greatermekong.org/greater-mekong-subregion-rural-no-more (accessed September 2019).

B. The Greater Mekong Subregion Program Strengths, Weaknesses, Opportunities, and Threats Analysis

35. A snapshot of the current state of the GMS Program provides a further rationale to address weaknesses, build on strengths, and turn potential threats into new opportunities.

36. GMS-2030 will build on the subregion and Program strengths, with a focus on selectively seizing transformative opportunities to address new economic, social, and environmental demands. This will require policy and knowledge solutions to further integrate the GMS and position it to respond to a changing world.

Box 2: Strengths, Weaknesses, Opportunities, and Threats (SWOT) Analysis of the Greater Mekong Subregion Program

Strengths

- Greater Mekong Subregion (GMS) countries have done well in tackling the health impacts of COVID-19
- Strong country ownership and leadership, supported by well-functioning processes and institutions
- Goodwill and group pride based on demonstrated results
- Sharp focus, especially on connectivity and corridor development
- Convening power: established forums, dialogue, learning and knowledge exchange
- Alignment with national priorities
- Bedrock of owned, high-priority projects as the basis for financing
- A strong brand and firm Asian Development Bank commitment

Weaknesses

- Overall approach needs revision to address the new development challenges holistically
- Insufficient integration across sectors and themes
- Program is overly public sector oriented, with limited participation from the private sector, civil society, and local representatives
- Knowledge and policy dialogue needs sustained attention and resources
- Mixed implementation in the critical areas of trade and investment facilitation and digital solutions
- Slow progress in implementation of the Cross-Border Transportation Agreement
- Weak health care systems

Opportunities

- Respond to widely expressed new demands such as (i) technology, (ii) green growth, (iii) health, (iv) livable cities, and (v) migration
- A strong private sector partnership will yield dividends; projects to explore catalyzing private financing
- Establish thought leadership on a few selected themes, collaborating with GMS think tanks, academia, and experts
- Actively market the GMS platform to attract other development partners to facilitate coordinated approaches to knowledge and projects
- Respond to growing public awareness and support for biodiversity conservation and "One Health" approaches

Threats

- Slowdown of world and subregional economies due to COVID-19
- A slowing global economy may shrink the resource envelope and weaken value chains
- Inequality, poverty, and social and economic exclusion may sap support from agreed programs
- GMS suffers from air, water, and land pollution, due to severe climate change impacts
- Threats of global or regional pandemics
- Unsustainable growth may destroy natural capital of the GMS

COVID-19 = coronavirus diseases.
Source: ADB GMS Secretariat.

II. Vision and Mission Statement

37. The GMS-2030 Vision is to develop a more integrated, prosperous, sustainable, and inclusive subregion.

38. To achieve the Vision, GMS-2030 establishes a Mission Statement for the GMS Program: a subregional cooperation program focused on its fundamental strengths of community, connectivity, and competitiveness while embracing the core principles of environmental sustainability and resilience, internal and external integration, and inclusivity, for building a GMS community with a bright shared future. The three core principles are explained as follows.

39. **Environmental Sustainability and Resilience.** GMS countries recognize the need for environmentally sustainable, inclusive, and resilient economic growth for the subregion for effective recovery from the effects of the COVID-19 pandemic. Based on the GMS country commitments to achieve the United Nations Sustainable Development Goals (SDGs) and the goals of the Paris Agreement—and in view of the multiple challenges as a result of environmental degradation, vulnerability of the subregion's natural resources, climate change risks, and the devastation brought about by the COVID-19 pandemic—GMS countries agree to work together to ensure not only environmental sustainability and resilience in the subregion but also robust economic development. This core principle will be factored in every intervention under the GMS Program. The GMS Program will support more sustainable modes of transport such as railways; clean and efficient energy; sustainable agriculture and tourism interventions; joint management of water quality in oceans and rivers; responsive, inclusive, and equitable human capital development; and the development of a network of competitive, green, and livable cities.

40. **Internal and External Integration.** The GMS Program has achieved significant success in connecting and integrating the subregion since its establishment in 1992. In the next decade, the GMS Program will focus on

Environmental sustainability and resilience. The latest techniques in sustainability and crop yield are developed in the Southern Horticultural Research Institute in Viet Nam with support from the Asian Development Bank.

Internal and external integration. (above) GMS-2030 seeks to deepen integration among its member countries, while promoting integration of the GMS with other subregions.

Inclusivity. (right) The GMS Program seeks to include remote and unserved areas under the new GMS spatial strategic approach to reach low-income populations.

deepening integration among its member countries, while promoting integration of the GMS with other subregions in South Asia, Southeast Asia, and Northeast Asia. This core principle will lead to the expansion of the network of economic corridors, improvement of GMS border infrastructure and cross-border cooperation; development of ports, airports, and river transportation; increased integration in regional value chains beyond the GMS; diversification and increased complexity of GMS exports; increased efforts to facilitate trade and investment for a more competitive GMS; and a means to address external risks.

41.   **Inclusivity.** While there have been significant results from the GMS Program, having focused consistently on subregional growth and development, some segments of society (i.e., lower income populations, including a disproportionate representation of women) should benefit more from its future interventions. Furthermore, COVID-19 is likely to have long-term impacts on local economies and on vulnerable populations which, together with rapid and significant economic structural changes that take place in the subregion and beyond, will pose further challenges. GMS Program interventions will address these challenges to ensure that all citizens—male and female of all ages, social classes, and ethnic groups—will benefit. By adopting the principle of inclusivity, the outreach of the GMS Program will include remote and unserved areas, thus widening the economic corridor network, developing border zones, and linking cities to rural areas under a new GMS spatial strategic approach to reach low-income populations. The GMS Program also will develop and coordinate health services across borders to include unserved populations, such as ethnic minorities, migrants, and workers in special economic zones.

42.   The new core principles included in the GMS-2030 Mission Statement will be applied to all interventions under the Program. These will be reflected in the innovative approaches that will be adopted in GMS-2030, as well as infused across the pillars of the strategy.

Box 3:   Greater Mekong Subregion Support to the Sustainable Development Goals

The Greater Mekong Subregion Economic Cooperation Program Strategic Framework 2030 promotes regional cooperation initiatives to help individual countries deliver their United Nations Sustainable Development Goal (SDG) commitments. Many SDGs have transboundary elements that include air and water pollution, climate change, labor migration, transmission of communicable diseases, trade in goods and services, and cross-border infrastructure.

In coordinating efforts, GMS countries will leverage improvements in

SDG 1 (End poverty in all its forms everywhere)

SDG 2 (End hunger, achieve food security and improved nutrition, and promote sustainable agriculture)

SDG 3 (Ensure healthy lives and promote well-being for all at all ages)

SDG 5 (Achieve gender equality and empower all women and girls)

SDG 6 (Ensure availability and sustainable management of water and sanitation for all)

SDG 7 (Ensure access to affordable, reliable, sustainable and modern energy for all)

SDG 8 (Promote sustained, inclusive and sustainable economic growth, full and productive employment, and decent work for all)

SDG 9 (Build resilient infrastructure, promote inclusive and sustainable industrialization and foster innovation)

SDG 10 (Reduce inequality within and among countries)

SDG 11 (Make cities and human settlements inclusive, safe, resilient, and sustainable)

SDG 13 (Take urgent action to combat climate change and its impacts)

SDG 14 (Conserve and sustainably use the oceans, seas and marine resources for sustainable development)

SDG 15 (Protect, restore, and promote sustainable use of terrestrial ecosystems, sustainably manage forests, combat desertification, and halt and reverse land degradation and halt biodiversity loss)

SDG 16 (Promote peaceful and inclusive societies for sustainable development, provide access to justice for all, and build effective, accountable, and inclusive institutions at all levels

SDG 17 (Strengthen the means of implementation and revitalize the Global Partnership for Sustainable Development).

Source: ADB GMS Secretariat.

III. Innovative Approaches

43.   Though firmly grounded in its proven success areas of connectivity and its project-based approach—despite reflecting changing external circumstances—GMS-2030 will implement its Mission Statement through innovative approaches in six cross-cutting areas.[37]

A.   Harnessing the Digital Revolution

44.   The COVID-19 pandemic has highlighted the need to invest in digital infrastructure, and to shape policies and regulations to help the private sector digitalize, and improve access for all to government and payment services, as well as to e-commerce. These will be critical to a sustained and inclusive recovery. Harnessing the new possibilities opened up by digitalization is central to the efforts of the GMS to build a robust, regionally integrated economy in 2030—one that is better able to withstand a competitive external environment, is fully equipped to seize new opportunities, and is capable of addressing over the medium to long term the challenges of recovery and resilience against the economic and social damage to the subregion brought by the COVID-19 pandemic. GMS-2030 will chart a new course that will enable subregional cooperation to best realize these new opportunities as a result of the digital revolution, fueled by big data-based innovations that are unfolding and affecting nearly all parts of the economy, boosting productivity, and changing the pattern of production and work.

Investing in digital infrastructure. Internet cafés with fast and reliable internet connection are made possible through investments in digital infrastructure.

---

[37]   Some of the innovative approaches were identified in the GMS Ha Noi Action Plan 2018–2022 and are now included in GMS-2030.

Enhanced spatial approach to development. The new approach will exploit the agglomeration effects of urbanization, linking cities across borders through increased cross-border trade, rising tourism, and agriculture value chains.

45.   COVID-19 will likely act as a catalyst for digital transformation. Digital readiness has proven to be a crucial factor, allowing some GMS economies to successfully contain the spread of the virus and others to keep the economy relatively open during the pandemic. Developing the enabling infrastructure, nurturing a cooperative ecosystem, and building digital skills and education are all critical to support digital transformation. The GMS will exploit e-commerce potential to boost consumption and factor productivity at the firm level, generate exports, stimulate innovation, offer flexible and dynamic employment, and especially focus on benefits for MSMEs. E-commerce will play a strong role in raising consumption, given that firms' participation is associated with a 30% increase in productivity, and a 50% increase in exports. It confers particularly strong benefits on small firms in Asia (footnote 25). The PRC has made giant strides and leads in e-commerce, while Viet Nam is advancing rapidly. In other GMS countries, there remains a large unrealized e-commerce potential.

46.   Economic recovery post-COVID-19 in the GMS will require further liberalization in the trade of services and greater openness to foreign direct investment, bringing with them technological advances. Digital infrastructure across the GMS will comprise secure internet servers, high-speed broadband internet, and last-mile connections. Regulatory systems will be developed and harmonized, leading to efficiency gains and lower consumer prices, thereby enhancing export competitiveness in accordance with international law and all member countries' domestic laws and regulations. The GMS-2030 will focus on promoting trade and investment openness, skills development for women and men, and infrastructure investment in the digital economy, with GMS projects playing a key role in advancing the digitalization agenda as a cross-cutting theme.

47.   The subregion will target securing the gains from regional cooperation with the vision of open and well-integrated GMS economies with common standards and interoperability of systems. This is essential to maximize the benefits of trade and investment. A more harmonized regulatory environment will ease logistics and firm interactions, increase trade in goods and services, reap economies of scale in firm production, support e-commerce, and reduce fiscal leakages. A common GMS approach also will minimize the risks associated with digitalization: fragmentation of markets and local monopolies, cybersecurity and data vulnerability, lack of consumer protection, and labor market disruption. Such a common approach requires a well-articulated subregional strategy for an open,

integrated digital economy.[38] GMS-2030 will encourage subregional digital entrepreneurship in SMEs, noting that e-commerce has been shown to be a particularly powerful enabler of MSME growth. The GMS-2030 will promote peer learning and the exchanges of experiences through subregional forums and conferences.

48.   GMS-2030 will seek to realize the gains from digitalization through its projects, particularly those supporting information and communication technology infrastructure. In all sectors, project activities will be examined for the potential contribution of digital approaches and technologies that raise productivity. Linkages will also be established to determine the labor force skills, infrastructure investments, and regulatory reforms needed to support digital approaches. Digital innovations will also be encouraged as a guiding principle for productivity improvements in the agriculture sector and upgrading competitiveness in the tourism sector.

49.   GMS-2030 aims to create the GMS as an open platform for development partners and knowledge centers (see Section III-E) to address the manifold demands of the digitalization agenda, including learning from international experiences. Similarly, given the need to obtain private sector financing for infrastructure investments, as well as the close links between the willingness to invest and the regulatory and business environments, as well as fiscal regimes, the regional public–private dialogue will be critical (see Section III-D). The platform approach is suited to address these endeavors.

B.   An Enhanced Spatial Approach to Development

50.   GMS-2030 will deepen the spatial approach to development by expanding the network of economic corridors throughout the subregion, building upon existing transport corridors to maximize network effects and connections between corridors to promote growth and transform key corridor sections into full-fledged economic corridors. Economic corridors will stretch outside the GMS territory to connect with South Asia and other parts of East Asia to enable trade and investment. GMS corridors will connect people and businesses; link ports, cities, and centers of production to reduce logistic costs, and create efficiencies through climate-smart value chains across the subregion. The Economic Corridors Forum will continue to promote coordination, networking, and facilitation of initiatives to develop economic corridors in GMS.

51.   Development of economic linkages in border areas and between urban and rural economies will be a priority. The development of secondary roads and riparian transport and port systems will give impetus to economic activity within corridors, as will linkages to special economic zones and border economic zones. Thus, corridors will be widened to embrace the rural economy and prioritize the development of border areas, leading to the stimulation of SMEs. They also will act as powerful agents of inclusion by bringing into the regional market economy new economic actors from the rural and border economies.

52.   The new spatial approach will seek to exploit the agglomeration effects of urbanization, linking cities across borders through increased cross-border trade, rising tourism, and agriculture value chains. GMS-2030 will promote the establishment of a well-connected network of clusters of cities. The GMS Program will also prioritize multisector interventions in GMS areas that share common goods across borders.

---

[38]   World Bank. 2019. *The Digital Economy in South-East Asia: Strengthening the Foundations for Future Growth.* Washington, DC. http://documents1.worldbank.org/curated/en/328941558708267736/pdf/The-Digital-Economy-in-Southeast-Asia-Strengthening-the-Foundations-for-Future-Growth.pdf.

C.   A Deeper Dialogue on Policies and Regulation, Underpinned by Knowledge-Based Solutions and Capacity Building

53.   The needs and challenges of regional connectivity are changing due to growing economic sophistication, the fragmentation of production, and use of state-of-the-art technologies. The smooth flow of goods across borders, especially post-COVID-19, requires common logistics, customs standards and practices, and efficient transport and trade facilitation. Moreover, recovery from the pandemic over the medium and long terms will require GMS countries to move toward a freer flow of labor and investment, requiring policy understanding and common regulatory frameworks to protect and support the movement of goods and people. Establishing a regional energy trading market will require common standards and practices to allow the smooth transmission of power. So too, strengthening climate and disaster resilience requires addressing current and future risks through a system-wide approach, including its potential intersectoral and transboundary impacts. Policy dialogue, therefore, is essential in all GMS-2030 areas and it will be deepened to maximize the benefits of regional infrastructure projects and an integrated, subregional economy.[39] GMS-2030 will enable government officials to better develop regional policies and projects through participatory and consultative platforms.

54.   GMS-2030 will support policy and regulatory dialogue to increase reliance upon relevant knowledge-based solutions of increasing sophistication and complexity, tailored to the conditions of the subregion. Policy dialogue will take place at GMS summits, ministerial meetings, sector working groups, and thematic and sector forums. Knowledge sharing events to discuss policies among GMS countries and with other countries or subregions will be organized, such as the Policy Actions for COVID-19 Economic Recovery Dialogues in which GMS senior officials participated in 2020 to jointly brainstorm on responses to the pandemic.[40] In addition, the capacity building of GMS officials will be promoted under an enhanced Brunei Darussalam-Indonesia-Malaysia-Philippines East ASEAN Growth Area (BIMP-EAGA), Indonesia–Malaysia–Thailand Growth Triangle (IMT-GT), and GMS (B-I-G) Capacity Building Program. In many cases, off-the-shelf knowledge will have to be adapted to local conditions; in others, fresh research will be required, necessitating a careful nurturing of knowledge sources. The contributions of development partners and regional think tanks, such as the Mekong Institute, in tandem with the participation of project stakeholders, will play a vital role in this process.[41] The establishment of a GMS network of knowledge centers and think tanks will feed the GMS policy dialogue with local knowledge. This shift, leading to a deeper knowledge-based dialogue, will underpin the effort toward more holistic, responsive, and sustainable development solutions and a new willingness to consider transformative ideas.

D.   Embracing Private Sector Solutions

55.   In the medium to long term, GMS countries will attain ambitious growth and SDG commitments through expertise, knowledge, and financing that lie well beyond the capabilities of national governments or official development aid. Leveraging the knowledge and technical resources of the private sector, as well as its capital, will be critical to success. Apart from harnessing domestic or regional private sector talent and resources, foreign direct investment will play a much larger role in the GMS.[42]

---

[39]   Policy, regulatory, and technical dialogue will take place at all levels (i.e., leaders, ministers, senior officials, and sector working groups).

[40]   ADB. 2020. Technical Assistance Report on Policy Advice for COVID-19 Economic Recovery in Southeast Asia. Manila. www.adb.org/sites/default/files/project-documents/54219/54219-001-tar-en.pdf.

[41]   It is envisaged that the Mekong Institute will coordinate a network of GMS academic institutions and think tanks to provide policy analyses and knowledge contributions to the GMS agenda.

[42]   Communiqué of the Group of 20 finance ministers (2017) that approved a set of principles providing international financial institutions with a framework for increasing private investment to support country development objectives. G-20. 2017. Communiqué. G20 Finance Ministers and Central Bank Governors Meeting, held in Baden-Baden, Germany. 17–18 March. www.g20.utoronto.ca/2017/170318-finance-en.pdf.

56.   In a changed world after COVID-19, the GMS Program will support countries to work with the private sector at the subregional level to prepare for this and other types of crises, including but not limited to diseases, disaster events, and climate change. GMS-2030 will seek to support the countries to develop a dynamic and innovative private sector that could contribute to and share the responsibility of tackling the subregional challenges posed by inequality, climate change, and other foreseeable and unforeseeable disasters. Such a private sector must be agile and inclusive, and excel in bringing benefits not only to its shareholders but also to the very people behind its successes—the men and women working in their organizations and supply chains, as well as those living in the communities within which the businesses operate.

57.   The GMS Program will shift toward a joint approach with the public and private sectors working together to promote sustainable development, with each project being scrutinized for its private sector financing potential. With greater attention to policy and regulatory reforms in the GMS work agenda, private finance will become an option for GMS countries that have not been able to access it due to an absence of appropriate regulations, institutions, or markets. In its project and knowledge work, the GMS Program will consider a spectrum of solutions, private as well as public, and will assist countries to access a variety of financing options. Thus, the private sector will not only be involved in financing but also in knowledge and the transfer of technology, especially relating to infrastructure projects. GMS-2030 will focus on the inclusive skills development of the labor force to meet the needs of the 4IR.[43] This is a topic of particular importance for the GMS, given labor mobility, and it will require significant participation from the private sector.

58.   GMS-2030 will enhance the role of the GMS Business Council and organize private sector forums in collaboration with the sector working groups on environment, agriculture, energy, health, transport, tourism, and other relevant sectors and themes. New sector or thematic taskforces will be established, with strong participation from the private sector, when required. The GMS Freight Transportation Association will be more actively engaged in promoting logistics and connectivity. A strong regional cooperation focus will be promoted in all these initiatives. GMS-2030 will seek to create opportunities for the public sector to better understand the issues and relevance of the regional private sector and to catalyze limited public sector financing to attract private sector funding into GMS projects.

E.   The Greater Mekong Subregion Program as an Open Platform

59.   The rising importance of working together across borders and the need to involve an entire range of diverse stakeholders from central and local governments, private and public sectors, academia, civil society, and development partners is a reflection of the growing sophistication of the GMS and has been further highlighted by the COVID-19 pandemic. GMS-2030 will seek to utilize the talents of all its stakeholders during its implementation.[44] The GMS Governors' Forum will be reinvigorated for more effective multisector and spatial coordination to take into account the interests of diverse stakeholders at the provincial level, as well as the private sector, in each country. The GMS Governors' Forum may support, as required, corridor-specific or bilateral forums where provincial governors and the local private sector, in contiguous areas, have common interests or challenges. Local governments will be beneficiaries and implementors of spatial strategies and projects. The active participation of local governments and local nongovernment and civil society organizations will be sought in most initiatives.

60.   GMS countries have long recognized that engagement with development partners warrants elevated attention (footnote 5). GMS-2030 will offer an open and inclusive platform to all development partners to pool knowledge and financing. Development partners will be encouraged to participate in all the sector working

---

[43]   This will include upgrading the skills of women and allowing them to take advantage of the new and changing opportunities created in the subregion.

[44]   The key stakeholders in the GMS are the national governments of its member countries. Other GMS stakeholders include local governments, civil society and nongovernment organizations, academia, think tanks, and other knowledge centers across the subregion.

groups, knowledge-sharing events, and investment projects of the GMS Program,[45] in line with their comparative advantages and interests. Development partners will be encouraged to participate proactively in the RIF and to take the lead in assisting GMS countries in selected themes and sectors, as required.

61.   Under GMS-2030, the GMS Program will strengthen its collaboration and coordination with other RCI initiatives with which the GMS has had a long tradition of close cooperation, including the ASEAN, a longstanding partner.[46] The GMS Program will selectively translate the dialogue and policy initiatives of ASEAN and the cooperation mechanisms between ASEAN and PRC into projects and provide technical assistance for the generation, sharing, and application of knowledge. The GMS Program will further implement ASEAN agreements by developing knowledge networks, policy dialogue, advisory services, and capacity-building programs. The focus areas for cooperation will include, at least, transport connectivity and trade facilitation, tourism, agriculture, and the environment.

62.   The GMS Program will also work closely and selectively with other regional initiatives, with a core mandate of RCI including the Ayeyawady–Chao Phraya–Mekong Economic Cooperation Strategy; Lancang–Mekong Cooperation; the Cambodia–Lao PDR-Myanmar–Viet Nam Cooperation (CLMV); and other regional cooperation frameworks. It will also extend collaboration with other RCI initiatives from outside the subregion, including the South Asia Subregional Economic Cooperation, Central Asia Regional Economic Cooperation, Bay of Bengal Initiative for Multi-Sectoral Technical and Economic Cooperation, and Indonesia–Malaysia–Thailand Growth Triangle, with a view to encouraging the implementation of high-quality and sustainable infrastructure projects.

63.   GMS countries will continue to accelerate enhancing links and synergies between the GMS Program and the Belt and Road Initiative to foster mutually beneficial and high-quality cooperation. This is based on the principle of extensive consultation, joint contribution, and shared benefits with a view to achieving high-standard, people-centered, and sustainable development.

64.   GMS countries are committed to sustainable development of the GMS through full implementation of the UN 2030 Agenda for Sustainable Development. GMS-2030 will pursue innovative, coordinated, green, and inclusive development in achieving sustainable development in the subregion. GMS-2030 will stress the importance of full implementation of the Paris Agreement at regional and national levels.

F.   Greater Mekong Subregion Program Results Framework

65.   The GMS Secretariat, in close coordination with GMS countries, will prepare a sound results framework to trace the implementation of GMS-2030 and its progress toward achieving the vision and program mission. The framework will monitor and steer the strategy, and will itself be supported by detailed sector-specific results frameworks that will be developed by the respective GMS sector working groups. The GMS Secretariat will provide guidance and support to the process of developing the sector results frameworks.

---

[45]   Under GMS-2030, a new RIF will be prepared. For details, see paragraph 134.
[46]   ASEAN and the GMS Program have already collaborated in certain areas, such as transport and trade facilitation, and there is great potential to expand this cooperation to other areas such as tourism and agriculture, as well as to accelerate the establishment of the ASEAN Economic Community and implement the free trade area agreement between ASEAN and PRC in GMS countries using the GMS program.

IV. Pillars of the Strategy

66. GMS-2030 will build on the successes of the Program and will retain the three pillars: Community, Connectivity, and Competitiveness. In view of the new challenges and emerging trends, GMS-2030 will particularly expand the Program's efforts to scaling up interventions under the community pillar, as well as being open to working in other areas in a flexible manner.

A. Community

67. Developing a strong GMS community, reflective of the strengths and opportunities of the human capital across the subregion, is essential to secure sustainable and inclusive development. GMS-2030 will promote a healthy and environmentally sustainable GMS community in which the well-being of all citizens is pursued. The COVID-19 pandemic has placed hygiene, clean and safe environments, and effective coordination across national health systems at the center of disease prevention. COVID-19 has highlighted the need for effectively dealing with the increasingly complex and harmful interactions between humans and wildlife that is exacerbated by biodiversity loss and climate change. GMS-2030 will support an inclusive, participatory, and equitable approach to building a subregional community in which men and women, young and old, of all ethnic and religious groups may work together to achieve sustainable development. GMS-2030 will support the countries to protect and enhance women's job and income prospects by acknowledging their roles in the informal and formal sectors, upgrading their skills, and supporting programs that will enable them to take advantage of the new challenges and changing opportunities created in the subregion during the crisis.

Health security linked to regional cooperation and integration. As governments lift COVID-19 restrictions, countries need to strengthen public health preparedness.

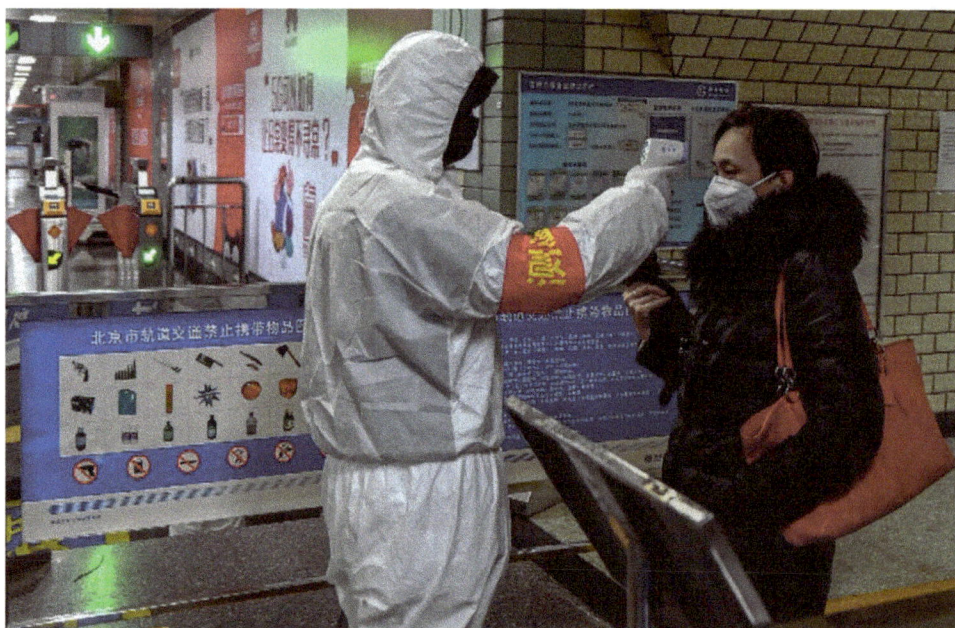

Shifting to the intermodal approach in the transportation sector under GMS-2030. (above) The approach will require new intermodal links and connections that will promote transport efficiency and lower costs.

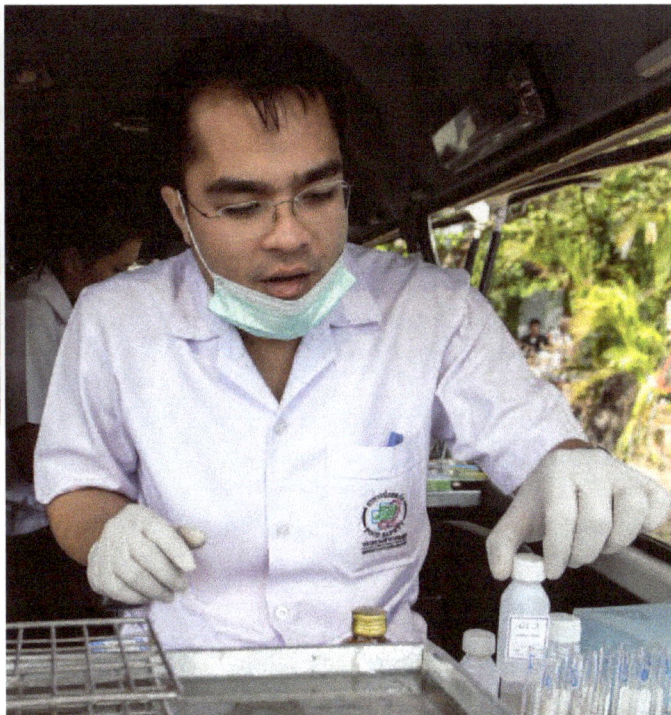

Promoting food safety and quality to international standards. (right) A Thai government technician is evaluating organic vegetables being grown by farmers.

1. Health

68.   The subregion continues to experience a high incidence of communicable diseases and drug-resistant microorganisms. GMS countries also suffer from inefficient health systems due to a lack of synergies and economies of scale and scope, and there are few joint solutions to common health problems. The GMS Health Cooperation Strategy aims to find collective solutions to common regional health problems and ways to supplement the limited resources for regional health investments that are considered a lower priority compared to national investments.

69.   Regional public goods feature strongly in the GMS health agenda, with a focus on communicable disease control through cross-border surveillance and modeling, information exchange, implementation of international health regulations, and pandemic preparedness. Global and regional public health threats are well known in the subregion, which has been affected in the past by the transmission of emerging, reemerging, and epidemic-prone communicable diseases. The cross-border spread of disease is a serious regional economic and health challenge for the subregion.

70.   Recognizing the potential threat to health security linked to RCI in the subregion, the GMS Program has supported strengthening countries' health system preparedness in order to respond to public health threats, such as COVID-19. The purpose is to advance each country's progress toward compliance with the World Health Organization's International Health Regulations and the requirement that national health systems develop core capacities to respond to public health threats of national and international concern.

71.   Support for the health sector under GMS-2030 will be structured in three pillars: the first promotes health security as a regional public good through a strengthening of core capacities for inclusive national health systems, developing a "One Health" response that takes a unified view of animal and human diseases and their interactions, and upgrading cross-border cooperation instruments. The second will address the impacts of labor mobility and greater connectivity, particularly on men and women within vulnerable communities; strengthen border health

systems and migrants' health; and provide health assessments of urban development and connectivity under GMS activities. The third will build human resource capacity in the subregional context.

72.   GMS-2030 will support the integration of health services throughout the subregion over the long term. As trade in health services expands due to improved connectivity, advances in digitalization and distance healthcare, and the growing demand from rising incomes, GMS-2030 will support the establishment of an enabling environment for trade in health services. This will include close collaboration by the public and private sectors and will be based on interoperability, uniform standards, regulatory convergence and enforcement, and a secure payments framework. This may require subregional agreements on the foreign or private ownership of health facilities. Portability of health financing across GMS countries, including financial protection and health insurance systems, is an important issue.

73.   The subregion also faces a continuum of risk factors associated with noncommunicable diseases (mainly cardiovascular, chronic respiratory, diabetes, and cancer), leading to increased morbidity and mortality. The GMS-2030 health agenda will underpin the sharing of evidence-based good practices on the different needs of and risks to men and women, as well as the cost-effectiveness of interventions for the prevention and control of major noncommunicable diseases.

74.   In response to the threat of global or regional pandemic outbreaks (e.g., avian influenza, African swine fever, Zika fever, Severe Acute Respiratory Syndrome, and COVID-19), GMS-2030 will retain focus on heightened preparedness to prevent, detect, and respond to public health threats, principally through surveillance and information systems, quarantine facilities, animal disease control zones, cross-country cooperation, diagnostics and laboratories, and capacity building. It will build strong alliances with other development partners and regional institutions such as ASEAN, consolidating health security as a regional public good. Intraregional and multisectoral collaboration under the "One Health" policy will enhance country efforts to attain SDG targets. The GMS Program will enhance cooperation among countries to limit the negative impact of the pandemic through joint research, policy dialogue, sharing experiences in treatment and prevention, and building capacity to address emergent health threats with cooperation in production and fair access to vaccines and medicines.

75.   In all new health initiatives, sustainable adaptation to, and mitigation of, the impact of climate change on health will be an essential dimension. Climate change is projected to affect health profoundly through various channels, such as agriculture, nutrition and water, livelihoods, and incomes. The impact on migration will be severe. Health sector interventions under GMS-2030 will support inclusion, as well as address the needs of vulnerable communities, including women's reproductive health. Health initiatives under GMS-2030 will address gender gaps and inequalities alike in access to and provision of health services. Collaboration with other sectors impacting health outcomes will also be considered, including the following areas: (i) road safety; (ii) indoor and outdoor air pollution; (iii) wildlife trade, as a key measure toward a "One Health" approach to reduce the risk of future disease outbreaks and biodiversity conservation; (iv) water and sanitation; and (v) digital health solutions and telemedicine.

76.   GMS countries are committed to cooperation on public health under the framework of the GMS Program. With the participation of the business community and relevant stakeholders, cooperation will center on health as a regional public good, with a focus on common information bases, prevention measures, and rapid response capabilities. New alliances between the private and public sectors will contribute to improved preparedness, modeling, and response.

2.   Environmental Sustainability and Climate Change

77.   Women and men across the subregion, including ethnic groups, play an important role as stewards and caretakers of natural resources, possessing extensive knowledge of seasonal variations, as well as historic patterns and traditional management systems. Furthermore, local communities, particularly poor communities, disproportionately bear the burden of severe climate-related events.

78.   GMS-2030 will support the policy, planning, and safeguards that relate to biodiversity conservation, pollution control and remediation, waste management, and a low-carbon transition. It will enhance resource efficiency by promoting sustainable consumption and production. GMS-2030 will address pollution by expanding green business development via markets for environmental goods and services and mobilizing private sector resources. It will support knowledge products to develop (i) inclusive policy frameworks and land resource planning in natural resource management and ecosystem services, (ii) financing policies to benefit distribution mechanisms for ecosystem services, (iii) measures to de-risk investments and promote private investment, and (iv) regulatory frameworks and standards for climate-resilient infrastructure. GMS-2030 will support measures to conserve biodiversity corridors in the subregion, building from the current sector strategy and action plan.[47]

79.   COVID-19 has strong links to environmental sustainability and climate change, with the origins of the pandemic traced to increasingly complex and harmful interactions between humans and wildlife, exacerbated by biodiversity loss and climate change. Furthermore, human vulnerability to the pandemic itself is associated with pollution, as people living in areas with high air and water pollution are more likely to have compromised respiratory and cardiac systems and are therefore more vulnerable to the impacts of pandemics. Employing a systems approach and holistic thinking in the implementation design of post-pandemic recovery and stimulus packages is critical. To achieve this, GMS-2030 will support, post-pandemic, the green and resilient recovery efforts of GMS countries in the medium and long terms. In the medium term, GMS-2030 will (i) support policies to build holistic community resilience, rebuild livelihoods, and create jobs without compromising ecosystem integrity; (ii) promote investments in cleaner air, water, and soil through the facilitation of low-carbon transitions in the energy, transport, and agriculture sectors; and (iii) demonstrate digital and spatial technologies to accelerate recovery from the pandemic. In the long term, GMS-2030 will (i) promote nature-based solutions to sustainably manage landscapes, cityscapes, seascapes, and wildlife; (ii) reduce supply chain risks and vulnerabilities to future pandemics by promoting resilient infrastructure in key sectors; and (iii) enhance capacities to mobilize innovative green and blue financing.

80.   Given the severity of climate change threats to the subregion, GMS-2030 will treat climate as an important consideration of GMS activities, with detailed interventions in each sector. GMS-2030 will also catalyze private capital based on the scale of financing needs.[48] The four key directions to successfully address climate change under GMS-2030 are (i) ensuring proactive adaptation and resilience-building measures with a strong regional dimension in sectors that demonstrate their benefits;[49] (ii) advancing resilience in all its dimensions, including physical, ecological, financial, social, and institutional; (iii) mitigating greenhouse gas (GHG) in line with the goals of the Paris Climate Agreement; and (iv) strengthening financing and enabling policy environment prospects.

---

[47]   ADB. 2017. *Greater Mekong Subregion Core Environment Program. Strategic Framework and Action Plan 2018–2022.* GMS Core Environment Program. Bangkok. https://greatermekong.org/sites/default/files/CEP-Strategic-Framework-2018-2022-web%20version.pdf.

[48]   Supports SDG 13 on climate action, SDG 14 on life under water, SDG 15 on life on land, and SGD 12 on responsible consumption (disposal of plastics).

[49]   Recent estimates by the Global Commission on Adaptation show that investing $1.8 trillion globally in five climate adaptation areas—strengthening of early warning systems, making new infrastructure resilient, improving dryland agriculture crop production, protecting mangroves, and making water resource management more resilient—from 2020 to 2030 could generate $7.1 trillion in total new benefits.

81.   GMS-2030 will strengthen climate and disaster resilience by addressing key vulnerabilities in agriculture, industry, and tourism supply chains. Similarly, it will support climate-resilient road transport, energy systems, and urban infrastructure. GMS-2030 will focus on the resilience of water resources, including the Mekong River and other river systems in the subregion, as well as coastal and marine resources. Adaptation efforts will include nature-based solutions such as green infrastructure; landscape-based conservation approaches, including mangrove protection, afforestation, and protected area management; and strengthened community resilience through the adoption of inclusive approaches. GMS-2030 will explore the potential of developing investments with the primary purpose of resilience. Policy dialogues on adaptation and disaster risk reduction will be coordinated through a GMS-wide participatory platform that will engage people across the subregion actively managing natural resources, both formally and informally.

82.   GMS-2030 will mitigate GHGs with a clear-sighted and determined approach on energy efficiency and renewable energy, and a view to achieving a low-carbon transition—focusing on policies to remove disincentives such as subsidies on fossil fuels—as well as supporting carbon markets. This will require a shift in transport toward railways, waterways, and green freight, as well as toward policies on urban transport within the ambit of green cities and policies on pollution standards and solid waste management. GMS-2030 will encourage cooperation in management of urban and industrial wastewater along the Mekong River.

83.   Healthy oceans and river systems are critical for the GMS, given its high dependence on marine and river ecosystems. GMS-2030 will center on an inclusive and sustainable blue economy and improving livelihoods by (i) developing sustainable and resilient tourism, fisheries, coastal resources, and green port infrastructure; (ii) addressing pollution; and (iii) protecting and restoring key marine ecosystems and river basins. These activities will rely on several factors including high-level and digital technologies, especially in terms of pollution; improved environmental governance; coastal and marine resource management; and sustainable and innovative financing.

84.   GMS-2030 will pilot financing options such as payment for ecosystem services. It will support GMS countries to benefit from the ASEAN Catalytic Green Finance Facility under the ASEAN Infrastructure Fund. GMS-2030 proposes a concerted effort to address land, air, and water pollution, including plastic pollution from source to sea.[50] Over the initial GMS-2030 period, action plans—led by the GMS country governments with private sector participation in operations and implementation—will be developed on a regional basis. Technical support will develop investment projects and knowledge solutions, and financing will be obtained through partnerships.

85.   Under an enabling environment for climate change, GMS-2030 will promote climate risk and adaptation assessment studies and policy impacts, in addition to strengthening early warning systems. It will seek to widen the net for risk financing in order to strengthen safety nets for the most vulnerable communities and increase capacity building.

86.   An ambitious climate change and environmental sustainability program is crucial, given the vulnerability of the GMS. GMS-2030 provides a long-term sustainable development path for the subregion, which will be highly inclusive in protecting livelihoods, particularly in view of the links between environmental pollution and its risks to health.[51]

---

[50]   Supports SDG Target 2.3 (zero hunger) on agriculture productivity, SDG 13 (climate action), and SDG 15 (life on land [forests and biodiversity]).

[51]   The health effects of air pollution are serious. A significant number of deaths from stroke, lung cancer, and heart disease are due to air pollution. For more information, see www.who.int/airpollution/ambient/health-impacts/en (accessed June 2020).

B.   Connectivity

87.   The GMS Program will continue to support connectivity in a holistic sense, referring to the capacity of people—men and women of all ages, ethnic groups, and abilities—to access the products and services that they need to live healthy and productive lives. This will require an understanding of the connectivity needs across the GMS of individuals, groups of people, and businesses. Careful consideration of the different needs of transport users and consumers across the GMS will ensure the design and delivery of a responsive, safe, efficient, and sustainable transport infrastructure that will include an effective medium-term response to COVID-19.

88.   Likewise, across the GMS, energy usage at the household, community, national, and cross-border levels vary for several reasons including cost, purpose, volume, reliability, and efficiency. GMS-2030, in considering the energy needs across the GMS, will utilize time–use surveys that analyze how improved energy delivery can decrease poverty, which could unlock the human capital potential for sustained growth across the subregion. Furthermore, GMS-2030 will pilot and promote renewable and efficient energy, particularly in off-grid areas, to minimize the environmental impacts of service delivery.

1.   Transport

89.   GMS-2030 will advance the connectivity agenda in the subregion and build on the Program's strong record of investments in the transport sector. In line with the SDG aim of a resilient infrastructure, the Program will further enhance subregional transport infrastructure. The vision of a seamless, efficient, reliable, and sustainable GMS transport system[52] will be realized by the following:

(i)   The shift to an intermodal approach will encourage competition within and across corridors, and will require new links and connections (e.g., port–highway–railway connections). This is essential to gain transport efficiency and lower costs.

(ii)   Transport connectivity gains will be maximized via cross-border transport to create a single market and production base, with the free flow of goods, services, and labor in line with the Cross-Border Transport Facilitation Agreement objectives of cross-border movement of trucks, drivers, and goods without reloading or transloading, and coordinated management at and behind the border.

(iii)   Efficient logistics will require (a) improvements in infrastructure (i.e., transport and communications); (b) increased supply chain management capacity within shippers, traders, and consignees; and (c) well-developed regulatory and institutional frameworks. GMS-2030 will support investments in inland dry ports, logistics hubs, and inland container depots, and will foster close linkages with the private sector (e.g., freight transport associations) while building the capacity of relevant stakeholders.

(iv)   GMS-2030 will place a greater emphasis on asset management for efficiency and reliability reasons, and will ensure that the common performance standards underlying the regional corridor network are upheld by exploring a variety of financing options for maintenance (including fee-based); enhancing road management systems; and improving road maintenance work standards, with greater private sector participation and improved consideration of climate risk.

(v)   Given the disappointing GMS road safety record and its adverse impact on health services costs, GMS-2030 will aim for common road safety standards including road accident data collection, definitions for road accidents, standard procedures for reporting road accidents, and road safety database systems. It will also measure and evaluate outcomes, develop the capacity of road safety agencies, and ensure that safety engineering standards are default requirements. Education and enforcement to change behavior is

---

[52]   ADB. 2018. *GMS Transport Sector Strategy 2030: Toward a Seamless, Efficient, Reliable, and Sustainable GMS Transport System*. Manila. www.adb.org/documents/gms-transport-sector-strategy-2030.

critical.[53] With regard to the impacts of COVID-19, a decrease of congestion on road networks may result in higher vehicular speeds and thus more high-speed accidents. As such, GMS countries will especially need to aim for stricter education, enforcement, enhanced road safety capacity, and sufficient budget allocation for road safety.

(vi)   To facilitate the movement of people and goods, the GMS-2030 will encourage GMS countries to promote discussion on fast track priority lanes, eco-friendly lanes, and green channels.

90.   The GMS-2030 transport program will seek innovative strategies in six new areas, as follows:[54]

(i)   Regarding railways, given the greater potential arising from higher economic density in the GMS, strategies and master plans will emphasize private sector investment, concessions, maintenance, and operations. The organizational structure of the Greater Mekong Railway Association will be improved. In addition to a network strategy, an operational readiness plan will be developed. The GMS railway network would be integrated into the Trans-Asia Railway project. The shift toward railways will lead to environmental sustainability (reduced emissions); it also will integrate the GMS with Europe, Central Asia, Malaysia, and South Asia. By completing the missing links and upgrading capacity, railways will become a powerful force for inclusion.

(ii)   GMS-2030 will shift emphasis toward developing and expanding capacity in sea, river, and dry ports, given the growing importance of maritime trade. Greater port capacity and intermodal links will further strengthen GMS integration outwards. GMS-2030 will encourage the greening of ports to ensure healthy oceans and water bodies.[55]

(iii)   The promotion of inland waterways, coastal shipping, and passenger services, together with improved regulations, operations, and landside seaport access, will stimulate the rural economy, include underserved populations, and mitigate climate change.

(iv)   Post-COVID-19, noting the need for recovery in the aviation sector and the potential fast expansion in demand for air transport, GMS-2030 will promote international and secondary airports, as well as strengthen a regulatory regime that encourages greater private sector participation.

(v)   GMS-2030 will integrate transport into urbanization strategies and planning, particularly along corridor networks, and realize climate change benefits. To further support environmental sustainability, particularly in relation to air pollution, efforts will be undertaken to tap new technologies in the electrification of transport modes in the subregion.

(vi)   Considerations of the social, environmental, and resettlement effects of transport projects, as well as road safety, will be priorities under GMS-2030 and will contribute to more inclusion.

91.   While COVID-19 spread across the globe, GMS governments successively shut international borders at short notice, seriously affecting transport. In order to reopen cross-border transport, GMS-2030 will promote health, safety, and security requirements on public transport and non-motorized modes of transport in densely populated areas, including walking and cycling. The GMS Program will emphasize health and safety measures at construction sites, ensuring a hygiene-conscious design for GMS transport projects.

92.   The transport sector will remain central to GMS-2030. To reflect an evolving world and regional conditions, it will be infused with the core principles of sustainability, integration, and inclusion. Policy and regulatory dialogue

---

[53]   Supports SDG Target 3.6 on health and road safety.
[54]   Supports SDG 9 on resilient infrastructure.
[55]   ADB. 2019. ADB Launches $5 Billion Healthy Oceans Action Plan. News release. 2 May. www.adb.org/news/adb-launches-5-billion-healthy-oceans-action-plan.

will be key to developing intermodal approaches, logistics reforms, and initiatives in the new areas outlined, with the role of the private sector and of modern technologies placed at the heart of the dialogue. Notably, infrastructure services will critically depend on digital solutions. Given the vast agenda, the coordinated participation of development partners will be essential to success.

2. Energy

93. The GMS-2030 energy strategy aims to improve energy supply security and environmental sustainability through cross-border trade, and to promote clean and renewable energy. In fact, bilateral energy trade is taking place today in the GMS, and some power utilities already employ third-country transmission facilities. A GMS regional transmission master plan will be prepared, based on a comprehensive study of generation and transmission development opportunities for cross-border electricity trade among GMS countries. GMS-2030 will encourage the next leap in integration toward a wholly competitive regional market with multiple seller-buyer regulatory frameworks, requiring an operational Regional Power Coordination Center (RPCC) with supporting working groups on regulation, harmonized technical standards, and strategic planning and operations. Although an intergovernmental Memorandum of Understanding for the RPCC in the GMS has been signed by the countries[56] and regional grid codes are expected to be finalized soon, its full establishment is a major requirement for further progress.

94. GMS-2030 will shift incrementally toward greater private sector participation in cross-border regional power projects. Over the GMS-2030 period, new initiatives will center on clean energy[57] and incentives for greater private investment in clean energy. Under GMS-2030, energy forums will be arranged with the relevant agencies and the private sector to discuss issues such as clean energy technology solutions and public–private partnerships for clean and renewable energy in the regional context.

95. GMS-2030 will prioritize clean energy and energy efficiency as a part of the future energy agenda.[58] This will include sharing knowledge and technology solutions, as well as business models—including for small, mini, and micro-grid and battery storage solutions and last-mile connectivity in border and harder-to-reach areas. A capacity-building effort will promote higher penetration of clean energy and effective environmental management in the planning and implementation of power projects. Capacity building will be implemented through regional hubs (e.g., those for technological solutions for interconnections) for energy efficiency and renewable energy and for integrated resource planning for power systems.

96. GMS-2030 will thus reflect the three core principles: environmental sustainability; support for knowledge sharing on newer energy solutions, including hydrogen fuel, digital energy, ocean energy, solar and wind energy; and a regional energy efficiency framework. It will integrate the subregion and bolster energy trade prospects beyond the GMS, for example, by increasing the interconnection capacity between Malaysia and Thailand. It will rely upon intensive policy and regulatory dialogue in all these areas, based on best-practice knowledge, and will proactively adopt solutions with development partners and private sector assistance. Finally, GMS-2030 will embrace the participation of other development partners to address the increasingly complex regulatory and power trade agenda, as well as the heavy demand for investment in infrastructure and institutions.

---

[56] Cambodia, the Lao PDR, the PRC, Thailand, and Viet Nam signed the Memorandum of Understanding in December 2012, and Myanmar signed in June 2013.

[57] Defined as the combination of energy generated from renewable sources (e.g., sun, wind, waves, water, geothermal, biomass, or hydrogen fuels) and energy saved through efficiency measures.

[58] Supports SDG 7 (ensure access to affordable, reliable, sustainable, and modern energy for all).

C. Competitiveness

97. GMS-2030 will continue to improve competitiveness in the subregion through efficient facilitation of cross-border movement of people and goods and the integration of markets, production processes, special economic zones, and value chains. Transport and trade facilitation will continue to further advance the GMS Program, including customs reforms, coordination of border management, extending single-window inspection for goods traffic at selected border crossing points, and measures to enhance sanitary and phytosanitary (SPS) arrangements for GMS trade. Investment promotion within the subregion, along with foreign direct investment facilitated from outside the GMS, will move GMS countries into higher value chains. The GMS Program also will extend cooperation in agriculture, including food safety, trade modernization, and climate-friendly agriculture. Under GMS-2030, the tourism sector—adversely impacted by the pandemic—will focus on bouncing back from recession, with innovative strategies to continue developing the subregion as a single tourist destination, as well as offering a diversity of quality tourism products that could distribute benefits more widely and contribute to poverty reduction, gender equality, and sustainable development. Urban development will enhance competitiveness of the subregion by promoting GMS economic corridor towns and cities, as well as other priority urban centers and border points.

1. Trade and Investment Facilitation

98. COVID-19 has severely affected trade and investment in the GMS economies through disruptions to goods and services in the region's global value chains and a collapse in demand stemming from social distancing and lockdown measures. In the next decade, GMS countries will strengthen their efforts to keep their borders open and promote cross-border trade and investment within the GMS and with other subregions.

99. **Trade Facilitation.** The impressive gains in physical connectivity and transport facilitation and logistics need to be supported by trade facilitation to attain the full benefits of regional integration. The trade facilitation strategy, therefore, is directed at the core principle of tighter integration, including for trade beyond the subregion. This will be crucial to ensure post-pandemic recovery. It is also expected to affect inclusion, since easier border processes and greater use of electronic or digital communications will benefit the MSMEs that currently do not participate actively in regional trade. GMS-2030 will assist MSMEs to access more easily the greater regional and global market through the emerging trade pattern of e-commerce, online financial services, and electronic payment gateways.

100. GMS-2030 will accelerate facilitating cross-border trade and the full implementation of the Cross-Border Transport Facilitation Agreement. GMS-2030 aims to prepare the GMS to implement electronic customs transit systems that will be aligned to the requirements of the ASEAN Customs Transit System[59] or the TIR Convention.[60] A well-functioning subregional customs transit system will eliminate duplicate trade procedures and guide transshipments through customs guarantees and the like.

101. Customs modernization will be a key area under GMS-2030 in an effort to apply the provisions of the World Trade Organization Agreement on Trade Facilitation and the standards of the Revised Kyoto Convention of the World Customs Organization, using digital technologies and risk-based systems for compliance to realize efficiency gains. Institutional capacities will make use of time release studies to identify bottlenecks in the trade flow to improve the effectiveness and efficiency of border procedures by building skills in other customs core areas, such as risk management, advance rulings, rules of origin, and valuation. A greater emphasis will be placed on strengthening links with the private sector, such as in various customs compliance programs, with a move toward

---

[59] For GMS members that are also members of ASEAN.
[60] United Nations Economic Commission for Europe. 2012. Trade Facilitation Implementation Guide: TIR Convention. http://tfig.unece.org/contents/TIR-convention.htm.

an authorized economic operator program, a key driver for a solid customs–business partnership to secure and facilitate global trade, thus enhancing economic prosperity.

102.   GMS-2030 will encourage electronic customs clearance, digital tracking through technologies such as blockchain, on-board mass, and radio frequency identification. Investments and common standards in border-crossing infrastructure will be encouraged to include health screening and further improvements in customs, immigration, quarantine, and security.

103.   To coordinate border management, GMS-2030 will strengthen capacities in SPS measures, involving surveillance and inspection programs for plant and animal health, fisheries, and food safety, and in the management of processed foods. This will encompass full coordination—ideally through single-window arrangements—in customs, health, sanitary and SPS, veterinary, and other regulatory requirements. It will be directed especially at economic corridors where transport and trade performance will be monitored.

104.   GMS-2030 will encourage member countries to tighten cooperation under regional free trade agreements such as the Regional Comprehensive Economic Partnership and the free trade area agreement between ASEAN and the PRC, to accelerate the establishment of Electronic Origin Data Exchange System and the application of self-service printing of Certificate of Origin, to facilitate the implementation of regional free trade agreements, to help address tariff and non-tariff barriers, facilitate and promote the free flow of goods and services, enhance two-way investment, and maintain the integrity of supply chains. The smooth implementation of regional free trade agreements will mitigate the adverse impact of the pandemic, restore economic and trade confidence, and contribute to economic recovery. GMS-2030 will enhance member countries' ability to negotiate and implement free-trade agreements.

105.   **Investment Facilitation.** GMS-2030 will support easing constraints to the flow of investment within the subregion and foreign direct investment from outside the GMS, including diagnostic studies to examine the barriers to greenfield investments that may be in place. GMS-2030 will emphasize the kinds of investment that are most beneficial to GMS countries and which will have spillover effects and contribute significantly to moving GMS countries higher in value chains. GMS investment cooperation and investment facilitation will be based on the liberalization set up under the free trade area framework agreement between ASEAN and the PRC.[61] As appropriate, GMS-2030 will support the creation of an integrated investment market—covering direct (e.g., greenfield projects) and indirect investment alike, as well as portfolio investments through capital markets, including harmonization of standards and requirements, equity in fiscal treatment, avoidance of state aid and anti-competition measures, and equal treatment under corporate and other commercial laws. GMS-2030 will promote a well-connected GMS network of special economic zones to attract quality investment to the subregion and benefit local populations, particularly in border areas.

106.   To ensure that the subregion is truly competitive, and to assist in the pandemic recovery, GMS-2030 will encourage macro-level analyses on the barriers experienced by entrepreneurs, cooperatives, and MSMEs in access to finance, business development services, supply and value chains, and regional and international markets and networks. GMS-2030 will lay the necessary foundation for locally owned businesses to grow and prosper

---

[61]   The free trade area framework agreement between ASEAN and the PRC was signed in November 2002. It provides the legal basis for ASEAN and the PRC to negotiate further agreements leading to the creation of the trade area by 1 January 2010. The ASEAN Agreement on Trade in Goods was signed in November 2004, while the ASEAN Framework Agreement on Trade in Services was signed on 14 January 2007. To promote and facilitate investment flows, an investment agreement also was signed in August 2009. The ASEAN Comprehensive Investment Agreement stipulates key protection elements for fair and equitable treatment for investors, nondiscriminatory treatment on nationalization or expropriation, and compensation for losses. It also has provisions for transfers and the repatriation of profits in freely usable currency, and provides investors recourse to arbitration to settle investor–state disputes.

and national and regional products to gain market share internationally through the creation of inclusive and equitable conditions.

107.   The GMS-2030 will support efforts toward further integration beyond the traditional regional value chains, particularly by embracing the South Asian and East Asian markets. The subregion would look to further liberalize its trade and investment regimes, adopt measures to enhance productivity growth, diversify production and exports, build fiscal buffers, and move up the technology chain.

2.   Agriculture

108.   The GMS has a large, unrealized potential as a global supplier of safe and environment-friendly agricultural products. The strategy for the agriculture sector seeks to expand production and regional trade through the adoption of a value chain approach and by promoting food safety and quality to attain international standards.[62] GMS-2030 will expand the sector by leveraging economies of scale to low transaction costs and harmonizing standards.[63]

109.   GMS-2030[64] will cover three main themes: (i) inclusive, gender-conscious agri-food value chains, and the financing of climate-friendly agribusinesses; (ii) crop and livestock safety and quality control systems; and (iii) agricultural adaptation in the context of the water–food–energy–climate nexus. Investment projects will support agro-industrial zones and parks, agribusiness incubators, livestock health and value chains, fisheries and aquaculture value chains, education and training, improved logistics, and incentives for innovation. These projects will recognize the often uncounted and undervalued contribution of women farmers in family-run farms and value chain activities.

110.   GMS-2030 will support climate-smart agriculture; promote climate-resilient production practices and technologies; and incentivize sustaining natural resources while mitigating GHG emissions wherever feasible. It will address climate change impacts on agricultural productivity—including through diminished water and soil quality—as well as food safety and quality. Since COVID-19 has adversely affected agricultural supply chains, GMS-2030 will support a food security response and recovery efforts in the medium and long terms. In the medium term, GMS-2030 will (i) strengthen agribusinesses to mobilize green financing in a post-COVID-19 context; (ii) formulate frameworks for green and resilient agricultural supply chain management, as well as a food safety risk assessment; and (iii) demonstrate digital technologies for food traceability and enhance post-pandemic resilience of agribusiness value chains. In the long term, GMS-2030 will (i) support agribusiness infrastructure and technology investments to support the viability and integrity of supply chains as well as reduce food insecurity, food loss, and waste; (ii) promote a "One Health" approach by reducing the environmental and human health impacts of production and processing of crops and livestock in the GMS; and (iii) strengthen GMS countries to implement the ASEAN Guidelines on Promoting Responsible Investment in Food, Agriculture and Forestry to increase resilience and contribute to the mitigation of and adaptation to climate change, disaster events, and other shocks.

111.   GMS-2030 will align standards, policies, and guidelines in the subregion on good agricultural and animal husbandry practices; ensure compliance with SPS standards; promote efficiency of water and land use; and encourage climate-resilient practices such as a system of rice intensification, regenerative agriculture, integrated

---

[62]   ADB. 2018. *Strategy for Promoting Safe and Environment-Friendly Agro-Based Value Chains in the Greater Mekong Subregion and Siem Reap Action Plan, 2018–2022*. Core Agriculture Support Program Phase II. Manila. www.adb.org/sites/default/files/institutional-document/366456/gms-value-chain-strategy-siem-reap-action-plan.pdf.

[63]   These standards cover crops, livestock, and aquaculture; food safety and quality assurance; certification and accreditation agencies; quarantine procedures; and surveillance systems and laboratories.

[64]   Supports SDG 2 (zero hunger) on agriculture productivity, SDG 5 (gender equality), SDG 13 (climate action), and SDG 15 (life on land [forests and biodiversity]).

pest management, and agro-forestry. In so doing, GMS-2030 will support equitable access to and participation of male and female farmers, young and old, in these activities across the subregion. GMS-2030 will support specific measures on climate change adaptation and disaster risk management by mainstreaming these considerations in subregional projects, including in partnership with ASEAN and other regional cooperation initiatives.

112.   GMS-2030 will support the transformation of GMS agricultural and food systems through energy efficiency improvements and through a greening of the supply chain at all feasible linkages, management of waste, and use of biomass for energy generation. It will (i) promote efforts to reduce transboundary animal and zoonotic disease risks; (ii) ensure food safety; and (iii) strengthen livestock value chains and facilitate livestock trade through infrastructure investments, capacity building, and policy support, and production supply connections, especially between cross-border enterprises.

113.   GMS-2030 will focus on small-scale farmers—including women farmers—and small and medium-size agro-enterprises. To establish the subregion as a global leader in safe and environment-friendly agriculture products (SEAP), GMS-2030 will aim to expand the markets for SEAP of GMS small-scale farmers and agro-MSMEs. This will include ensuring that smallholders and MSMEs in the subregion are well integrated into regional and global value chains. The development of inclusive and sustainable value chains is critical to achieving the vision for the GMS to become a leading global supplier of SEAP. Smallholder farmers—including women farmers—and MSMEs are the predominant majority in the GMS agrarian structure. The supply of safe and high-quality food to increasingly demanding consumers in the subregion and globally is assured by organized and efficient value chains. GMS-2030 will therefore focus on integrating smallholders and MSMEs into value chains that are able to add value, assure safety and quality, and manage the logistics needed to take food from the field to the table.

114.   GMS-2030 will support GMS countries to take decisive steps toward environmental sustainability through reform of agricultural practices. These will include non-point source pollution and the nexus between agriculture and ocean health, fostering the application of digital technology, and increasing the role of agriculture in the renewable energy mix. Through stronger linkages with regional and global value chains and resulting higher exports, it will have powerful integrative effects.

3.   Tourism

115.   Tourism services have been strikingly successful in the GMS, with annual growth in recent years exceeding global and Asian averages. Preceding the pandemic, tourism contributed more than 12% to Southeast Asia's GDP. Prior to COVID-19, GMS tourism was booming, with close to 80 million international tourists in 2019 having spent approximately $100 billion. Travel and tourism in that same year contributed from 4.6% to 26.4% of GMS countries' GDP and employed millions of workers. GMS tourist arrivals and corresponding destination spending in 2020 declined by about 80% compared to 2019, with a prospective recovery in international tourism activity not expected until late 2021.

116.   GMS countries have responded to the COVID-19 pandemic by implementing measures to protect public health and help the tourism industry survive its worst downturn in generations. These measures include (i) disseminating timely and clear information on travel regulations and health advisories; (ii) ensuring fiscal, monetary, and training support for a broad range of travel and tourism enterprises, including MSMEs; (iii) implementing social protection programs to safeguard formal and informal tourism workers' incomes and livelihoods; (iv) enacting stringent health and safety regulations for key tourism subsectors; and (v) providing monetary incentives to energize domestic tourism ahead of a reopening to international visitors. The GMS Program also organized several knowledge events to share recovery planning experiences and policies for rebuilding tourism in a more sustainable and resilient manner in the wake of COVID-19.

117.   GMS-2030 will support medium-term local and international tourism recovery initiatives. These will depend on how other parts of the world manage the pandemic. GMS-2030 will initially promote intraregional tourism. GMS countries will open to visitors from select countries based on their own pandemic prevention and control policies and if epidemiological evidence demonstrates that the community transmission of COVID-19 in these countries is subject to control and testing, surveillance, contact tracing, and that the health facilities in the origin and destination countries are adequate. Upgraded health screening infrastructure and information technology to support testing, surveillance, and tracing will be widely deployed during this time. GMS-2030 will emphasize the subregional nature of such policies, procedures, and infrastructure upgrades, and will ensure adequate coordination by the GMS working groups and national secretariats. A new GMS tourism marketing strategy and action plan will be implemented during this period, anchored on recovery.

118.   GMS-2030, over the long term, envisions a shift toward higher value-added sustainable tourism with longer stays and the inclusion of secondary destinations. ASEAN has taken the lead in certain areas by granting mutual recognition to tourism professionals and setting regional standards for service quality, clean cities, and green hotels. These initiatives and new health and hygiene travel protocols should be accelerated. GMS-2030 will involve the private sector increasingly in infrastructure development, standards implementation, and technology deployment. The Mekong Tourism Forum's role as a venue to foster dialogue and cooperation between the public and private sectors will be expanded.

119.   GMS-2030 will support the following strategic directions in the tourism sector, building on the current strategy:[65]

 (i)   Human resource development to lift tourism management capacity and improve service quality;

 (ii)   Connectivity investments to expand airports, secondary roads, railways, and ports;

 (iii)   Integrated destination management planning, including crisis management, secondary destination infrastructure investment, and implementation of common tourism standards to improve resilience;

 (iv)   Marketing and promotion of the GMS as a quality and safe multicountry destination to attract high-value travelers;

 (v)   Equitable participation of women and men to be assured in high-value product and service delivery;

 (vi)   Strengthen public–private linkages in all aspects of tourism, while emphasizing sustainability;

 (vii)   Strengthen public sector management to facilitate regional travel, implement air services agreements consistent with the free trade area framework agreement between ASEAN and the PRC, address tourism policy gaps, improve border facilities and management, and establish and enhance systems to collect tourism taxes and fees for reinvestment in inclusive and sustainable tourism initiatives; and,

 (viii)   Increase of cross-sector collaboration between tourism and other sectors, including cross-attendance in working group meetings, convening cross-sector thematic groups, and knowledge sharing.

120.   GMS-2030 will increasingly focus on strengthening crisis management capacity across GMS countries. The GMS is vulnerable to extreme weather and disaster events, and, as demonstrated by the COVID-19 pandemic, communicable disease outbreaks. Apart from immediate destination-wide losses, factors that slow recovery from crisis-induced downturns are low levels of preparedness and response capacity. This includes inadequate risk assessment, insurance, emergency management planning, and crisis communication.

65   Mekong Tourism Coordinating Office. 2017. *Greater Mekong Subregion Tourism Sector Strategy 2016–2025*. Bangkok. www.greatermekong.org/sites/default/files/2016_2025_GMS_Tourism_Sector_Strategy.pdf.

121. GMS-2030 will promote economic and trade integration via an expansion of tourism services, including intra-subregional tourism. The strategy will foster green urban infrastructure and sector-specific interventions in energy, transport, water, and land and coastal-zone management to reduce climate risks and pollution, including in water bodies and oceans. These efforts will make the GMS more livable for residents and visitors. Tourism's network of MSME supply chain linkages and entrepreneurs, including women and youth, will be expanded to raise incomes and boost inclusivity.

4.   Urban Development

122. The growing importance attached to urban development in GMS-2030 reflects the rapid pace of urbanization in the subregion; the critical role agglomeration effects play in driving growth, particularly in service-based activities; the utilization of digitalization and advanced technology as countries approach middle-income status; and the need to avoid constraints to growth, including negative externalities (i.e., congestion, pollution) that can arise if the urban agenda is neglected. Moreover, the linkage of major cities to economic corridors—at the heart of the GMS Program—and border areas is critical to ensure that connectivity investments yield the highest dividends.

123. The impacts of the global COVID-19 pandemic will make a mark on cities, physically and socially, that will echo for generations. COVID-19 has already significantly altered urban life. The fate of MSMEs and associated laborers that make urban centers work is uncertain. The GMS Program will focus on these changes and respond appropriately to current and future crises.[66]

124. In the medium term, cities will remain at the forefront to address the health and socioeconomic impacts of the COVID-19 pandemic. Building resilience of cities to future pandemics or similar types of crises requires a holistic approach. To achieve this, GMS-2030 will support the national strategies of GMS countries, focusing on (i) the enhanced use of digital technologies, including promoting information and communications technology to improve responses to pandemic situations, especially in terms of planning systems and services delivery; (ii) ensuring financial sustainability by enhancing the capacities of city authorities to mobilize innovative green and blue financing and build valuable partnerships with the private sector; and (iii) changing urban travel options and patterns by bringing in multimodal solutions such as mass transit systems, as well as rapidly shifting to investments in spaces for cycling and walking, as well as e-vehicles, along main corridors so as to offer people diverse mobility solutions.

125. In the long term, GMS-2030 will encourage holistic urban development[67] based on the current sector strategy.[68] It will aim to develop livable cities that combine gray, green, and blue infrastructure, with strategies to achieve not only an improved public health response, but also overall disaster and climate change resilience, thus ensuring that cities are more green, competitive, and inclusive. The planning and development of cities will encompass physical infrastructure, provision of essential services, recognition of the different needs and public service usage patterns of men and women, integrated urban transport, environmental protection, fiscal and financial foundations, and maximization in the role of the private sector to reap the greatest agglomeration gains. New planning approaches should bring open spaces, watersheds, forests and parks, and investments into corridors for cycling and pedestrian walking. GMS-2030 will support, within this context, the concept of green cities (as reflected in building codes, energy use and resilience standards, and urban transport) and of smart cities (to benefit from digitalization in basic service delivery, traffic flows, energy use, and climate resilience), with the final objective

---

[66] Van den Berg, R. 2020. How Will COVID-19 Affect Urban Planning? *The City Fix*. 10 April. https://thecityfix.com/blog/will-covid-19-affect-urban-planning-rogier-van-den-berg.

[67] Supports SDG 11 on cities (urban services, urban transport, and resilience) and SDG 6 on clean water.

[68] ADB. 2015. *Greater Mekong Subregion Urban Development Strategic Framework 2015–2022*. GMS Secretariat. Manila. www.adb.org/sites/default/files/institutional-document/173139/gms-urbandev-framework-2015-2022.pdf.

of developing inclusive livable cities. GMS-2030 will also support capacity development in urban planning and management.

126.   GMS-2030 will support a holistic approach to risk-sensitive regional planning, with a view to identifying, developing, and supporting interconnecting city clusters that will increase competitiveness and resilience, as well as benefit from economies of scale and agglomeration economies. This will encourage trade in services between cities to reflect gains from scale and specialization. Knowledge and good practices from successful twin city and cluster city concepts will be encouraged.

127.   GMS-2030 will prioritize the cities located close to rivers and seas with a concerted effort to address land, air, climate and disaster risks, and water pollution, including plastic pollution from source to sea through pollution control and waste management.[69] This will be important for environmental sustainability, as well as for disaster risk management and climate change mitigation and adaptation.[70] Initial focus will center on major cities located along the Mekong. GMS-2030 aims to support border area development for regional integration, equity, inclusiveness, and safety in the subregion, including realizing benefits from cross-border trade and labor migration. Urban–rural linkages and linkages across GMS cities will be promoted under GMS-2030 to integrate the GMS and ensure inclusion, and stimulate MSME production, especially in border areas.

D.   Other Areas of Cooperation

128.   In the coming decade, the GMS may face several new difficult-to-predict challenges that could affect economic development. GMS-2030 is designed to allow the Program to reposition itself to respond to these challenges via a flexible approach in which it encourages openness to working in new areas, including macroeconomic coordination; digitalization and new technologies; e-commerce platforms; logistics; labor mobility and safe migration; education and skills, including digital education of workers; and special economic zones. During the implementation of GMS-2030, GMS members may collaborate with relevant GMS stakeholders and consider developing initiatives in these areas by establishing knowledge forums, capacity-building programs, or task forces to respond to the new challenges, as well as maximize new opportunities in a rapidly changing environment. GMS-2030 will be closely aligned with the SDGs, and it acknowledges the intersectional impacts of gender inequalities across all priority areas, as well as the need for specific and integrated approaches alike for advancing gender equality and the empowerment of women, girls, men, and boys across the subregion. In addition, GMS-2030 will analyze the human capital constraints that face the subregion, with a particular focus on the gender-based stereotypes that limit 50% of the population from participating actively in, and benefiting directly from, development activities— whether sociocultural, economic, environmental, or political—culminating in the preparation of a GMS Gender Strategy as appropriate.

---

[69]   Supports SDG 14 on conservation and sustainable use of coastal and marine resources.
[70]   Supports SDG 11 on human settlement's resilience and SDG 13 on promoting planning that relates to climate change.

V. Institutional, Programming, and Monitoring Arrangements

129.   GMS-2030 aims to transform the GMS Program into a more strategic forum that will support high-level policy dialogue and regulatory harmonization in order to optimize infrastructure utilization that will be generated as a result of GMS projects.

A.   Institutional Strengthening

130.   GMS-2030 will continue to benefit from the well-established, multitiered institutional mechanisms of the GMS Program, with a triennial Summit of Leaders, annual ministerial conference, and frequent meetings of senior GMS country officials and sector working groups. GMS-2030 will strengthen the institutional framework of the GMS Program, while keeping it lean and efficient to allow it to respond effectively to emerging and more complex challenges of the next decade.

Revisions in the institutional arrangements will include the following:

• New sector working groups that will be established in critical areas, such as in trade and investment facilitation. A GMS private sector forum will be established to facilitate wider consultation on issues where the private sector has the highest potential to support economic growth, such as in digitalization or in investment facilitation.

• Greater flexibility to respond to new areas and emerging priorities included in GMS-2030, as well as proposed improvements in the RIF that will require changes in the terms of reference of sector working groups. New taskforces will be established as required and sector forums will be set up with private sector participation.

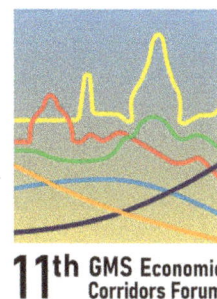

The GMS Program structure. The GMS Summit (every 3 years), the GMS Ministerial Conference, and the GMS Economic Corridors Forum (annual) are the main institutional structures of the GMS Program.

- Promotion of ministerial meetings in sectors where these are not already convened, in order to allow the Program to respond to new complexities, including challenges of policy and regulatory dialogue.[71]

- Support for dedicated sector secretariats for key sectors. For example, the Mekong Tourism Coordinating Office will be strengthened, and a Regional Power Coordination Center will be established to support sector working groups.

- Additional support to the GMS Governors' Forum and the Economic Corridors Forum for more effective multisector and spatial coordination to take into account the interests of diverse stakeholders at the national and provincial levels, including the private sector.

- Strengthening of the GMS Secretariat within ADB to support GMS-2030 implementation. The Secretariat will strengthen its knowledge, skills, and planning capabilities to ensure quality analytical work, leading to improved decision-making, formulation of sector strategies, and identification of subregional projects. Scenario development and strategies to deal with emerging risks will be of special relevance. The Secretariat may consider secondment of staff from GMS countries to broaden its talents and experiences.

- Additional support to the GMS national secretariats through greater staff stability, capacity, and resources for enhanced planning and coordination; and dedicated attention to GMS issues.

131.   GMS-2030 will support the establishment of a network of GMS knowledge institutes, universities, and think tanks, including the Mekong Institute, to prepare and disseminate knowledge products and services in the subregion. The GMS Secretariat will deepen partnerships and coordinate closely with development partners, think tanks, and universities in areas where their knowledge and expertise could be useful for the success of the Program and GMS.

B.   Strengthened Programming, Monitoring, Coordination, Partnerships, and Financing

132.   GMS-2030 will be supported by enhanced programming and monitoring systems in the GMS Program. Under GMS-2030, ADB as GMS Secretariat of the Program will deepen its support role as a knowledge provider, financier, and an honest broker. In close coordination with national secretariats and with other GMS stakeholders, the GMS Secretariat will play a greater role in curating knowledge, providing a unified public–private response to GMS activities, mobilizing financing for GMS projects, identifying and preparing projects, nurturing partnerships, and coordinating with other RCI initiatives. The GMS Secretariat, working with the GMS Sector Working Groups, will strengthen the implementation mechanisms for the GMS Program and ensure additional efforts to mobilize financial and advisory resources, especially from the private sector.

133.   The GMS Secretariat will continue to bring together GMS countries and focus on the regional dimensions of development. It will continue to coordinate GMS institutions, notably sector working groups. By working through national secretariats and focal points, the GMS Secretariat will support national capacity building in GMS countries and promote strong national ownership of the GMS Program. Capacity building of GMS officials also will be promoted under an enhanced BIMP-EAGA, IMT-GT, GMS (B-I-G) capacity building program.

134.   Under GMS-2030, a new RIF will be prepared. The RIF will retain its central role in developing a compendium of projects eligible for financing from a variety of public and private sources, placing greater emphasis on project quality, sustainability, and on advancing gender equality and social inclusion. Its project inclusion standards will

---

[71]   GMS ministerial meetings are regularly convened for the environment, agriculture, tourism, and the subregion's Cross-Border Transport Facilitation Agreement.

be revised and strengthened to increase its attractiveness to development partners and the private sector with respect to project readiness, economic and social returns, and adherence to good environmental and social practices and management standards. Each project will be encouraged to maximize the prospects of private sector financing through a variety of instruments. The role of development partners in de-risking projects to attract private investments will be explored. A new RIF Discussion Paper will be developed for deliberation.

135.   To ensure effective implementation of GMS-2030, a results framework will be prepared to monitor progress toward Program objectives, using proxy indicators and disaggregated data[72] against the key elements of the GMS Vision and Mission Statements. The results framework, assisted by a digital dashboard, will assess whether or not GMS-2030 is on track to achieve its vision and mission. It also will track SDG goal alignment. In consultation with the GMS countries, the GMS Secretariat will collect the data in the framework annually and report the results to GMS ministers and leaders. A review of the strategy will be undertaken at the midpoint of GMS-2030 implementation.

136.   The GMS Secretariat will support effective coordination, where required, between sovereign, non-sovereign (private sector), and public–private partnership teams that work on GMS projects. The GMS Secretariat will encourage blending policy reforms with private investments to unlock new sources of finance. In particular, the GMS Secretariat will expand financial channels for project investments and facilitate private sector and development partner financing. The positive spillover effects of regional projects should be magnified through greater private sector participation.

137.   As regional initiatives multiply and grow in ambition, the GMS Secretariat will continue to support regional and subregional strategic partnerships. The GMS Secretariat will continue to play the role of an honest broker, supporting the GMS countries to take advantage of new opportunities while preserving the Mission of the GMS Program and the Vision of the GMS.

---

[72]   Data will be disaggregated by sex, age, disability, religion, ethnicity, socioeconomic status, and other relevant demographic descriptors to ensure inclusive investment support—whether policies, programs, or projects—and equitable outcome.

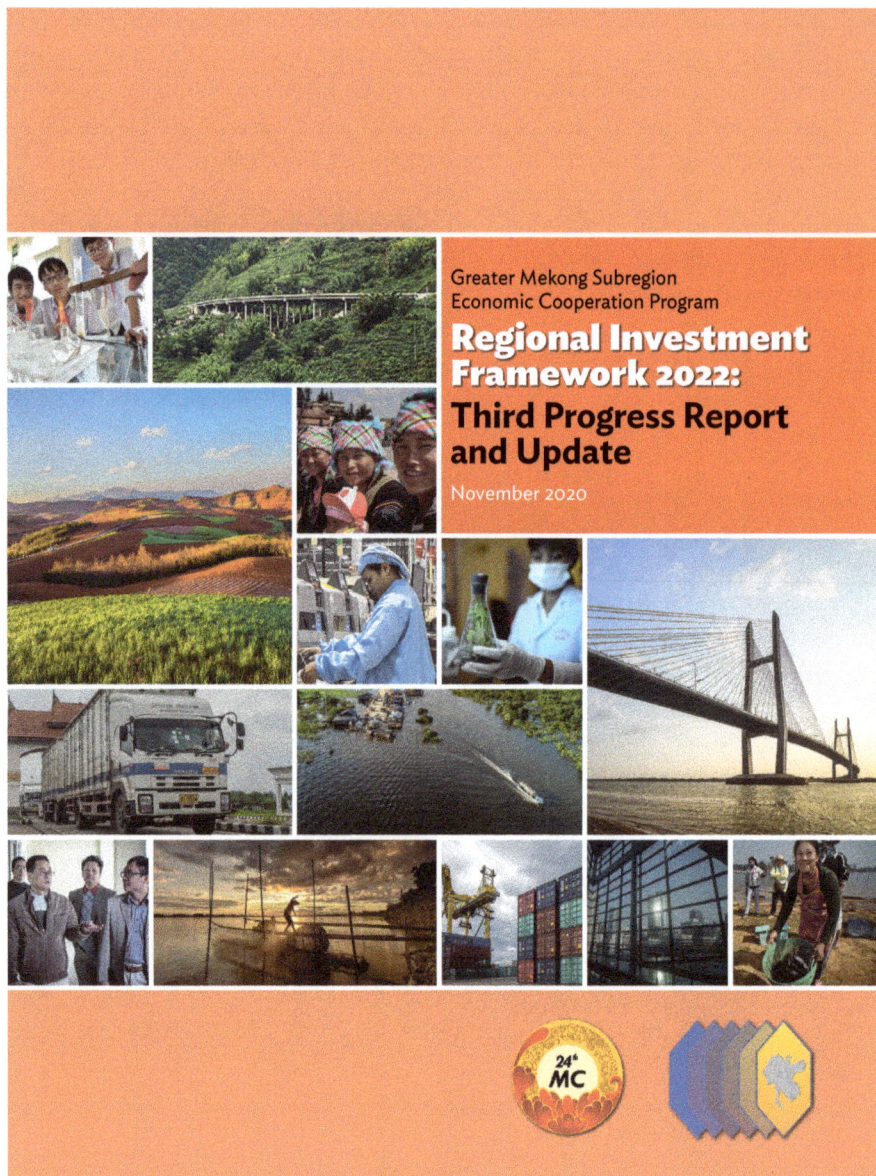

Greater Mekong Subregion
Economic Cooperation Program
**Regional Investment
Framework 2022:**
**Third Progress Report
and Update**
November 2020

The Regional Investment Framework 2022 Third Progress Report and Update. The Regional Investment Framework will be revised to raise the standard for project inclusion to increase its appeal to development partners and the private sector.

www.ingramcontent.com/pod-product-compliance
Lightning Source LLC
Chambersburg PA
CBHW050055220326
41599CB00045B/7421